Good Practice Guide: **Assessing Loss and Expense**

RIBA Good Practice Guides

Other titles in this series:

Adjudication, by Mair Coombes Davies

Arbitration, by Mair Coombes Davies

Building Condition Surveys, by Mike Hoxley

Employment, by Brian Gegg and David Sharp

Extensions of Time, by Gillian Birkby, Albert Ponte and Frances Alderson

Fee Management, by Roland Phillips

Inspecting Works, by Nicholas Jamieson

Keeping Out of Trouble, by Owen Luder

Marketing your Practice, edited by Helen Elias

Mediation, by Andy Grossman

Negotiating the Planning Maze, by John Collins and Philip Moren

Painless Financial Management, by Brian Pinder-Ayres

Starting a Practice, by Simon Foxell

Good Practice Guide:
Assessing Loss and Expense

Jeff Whitfield

RIBA ♯ **Publishing**

Published by RIBA Publishing, 15 Bonhill Street, London EC2P 2EA

ISBN 978 1 85946 445 8

Stock code 77529

British Library Cataloguing-in-Publication Data

A catalogue record for this book is available from the British Library.

Commissioning Editor: James Thompson

Project Editor: Neil O'Regan

Typeset by Academic + Technical, Bristol

Printed and bound by MPG Books, Cornwall

RIBA Publishing is part of RIBA Enterprises Ltd.

www.ribaenterprises.com

Series foreword

It is a fact of life that unforeseeable loss and expense claims will from time to time arise due to the complexity and longevity of architectural projects. The architect, acting as contract administrator, has a professional duty to the client to ensure that any such claims are correctly handled.

This Good Practice Guide provides everything you need to know to make fair evaluations of loss and expense. In clear, straightforward language, it explains why claims might arise, both under the contract and for breach of contract, their cause and effect, and their assessment and valuation by certifiers. It shows the importance of getting your certification right, and how claims may be avoided through the application of good procurement and contractual procedures. For any claims that do still arise, it outlines practical and pragmatic approaches to resolving them, either by yourself or through dispute resolution procedures.

Essential reading for all architects and contract administrators, this book will allow you to understand the principles of loss and expense evaluation yourself, so that you can undertake assessments safely, spend as little time as possible on them, and more time on getting on with the project.

Angela Brady
President, RIBA

Preface

In difficult markets contractors are expected to earn margins that were realistic in the boom years but which may now be out of reach. The problem is competition. In open tendering, contractors are obliged to price low to attract turnover and so the temptation is then to generate the required margins by seeking additional monies for every change in quantity, circumstance and in the programme. Under the JCT forms this method of recovery is either achieved by pricing variations or by the pursuit of loss and expense.

Architects have often steered clear of loss and expense claims in the past, preferring to leave the assessment of such claims to the quantity surveyor. This is unnecessary, because architects who understand the loss and expense process can enrich their project experience by ensuring that only those claims that are properly due under the contract are paid.

This guide arms the architect and contract administrator with all the knowledge necessary to make fair determinations of loss and expense, with the help of others and the cooperation of their client.

The guide concentrates on the use of JCT Standard Building Contract with Quantities 2011, sometimes abbreviated to SBC/Q 2011. Nonetheless, reference is made to NEC and to other forms of contract in recognition of the fact that the principles cited herein are transferrable across contract forms, seats of law and legal jurisdictions.

The base date for the book is October 2012 and all references are to the law prevailing at that date.

About the author

Jeff Whitfield is an expert witness quantity surveyor who practises in the UK and around the globe. Trained as a construction planner before training as a quantity surveyor, Jeff is a chartered surveyor and has a law degree. A member of the Academy of Experts for most of his 20 years' expert witness life, Jeff spent the first 20 years of his career on construction sites around the UK and Europe, culminating in his appointment as commercial director for a well-known international contractor.

Instructed on a variety of projects from airports to power plants, Jeff works mainly in the UK, the Middle East and the USA for contractors, employers and their legal representatives.

Jeff is the author of a number of books, including the predecessor to this volume, entitled *Loss and Expense Explained*, and is an executive director at Hill International UK, based in London.

Contents

Section 1
Basic principles

In this Section:

- *Introduction*
- *Reasons for claims*
- *Impartiality and independence*
- *Cost of conflict*
- *Claims avoidance*

Introduction

Construction projects are usually complex and unique. In manufacturing terms we might say that each building is a prototype. These complex prototypes generally need a considerable window of time for their completion; some require many months and some need years. When constructing a unique building over such a prolonged contract period, the need for change in the design is bound to arise and any change is likely to be accompanied by other delaying factors.

Naturally, the authors of construction contracts do their best to anticipate and provide for all those events that might possibly arise on a project. Additionally, the authors will have to draft amendments which become either necessary or desirable as the result of new legislation or the judicial interpretation of particular clauses. An example of this is JCT 2011, rewritten to comply with the legislation colloquially known as the new Construction Act but which is more correctly called the Local Democracy, Economic Development and Construction Act 2009.

Even with such careful amendments being incorporated, most contract forms inevitably fall short of perfection. Sooner or later an event or series of events will arise which falls outside the scope of the contract, or the judges will give a new and unexpected twist to the meaning of a particular provision. Any such occurrence will allow the affected party, usually the contractor, to seek additional remuneration by way of damages to take account of the changed circumstances under which the works are to be completed.

"Where a disruptive event is anticipated by the contract the contractor will need to seek reimbursement"

Where a disruptive event is anticipated by the contract – for example where a delay in the provision of design information causes the contractor to incur a loss – the contractor will need to seek reimbursement under the contract. In such situations where the contractor seeks additional monies, the document produced to encourage the employer to reimburse the contractor for the loss is often called a 'claim'. However, the term 'claim' is generic, descriptively vague and imprecise. So what does it really mean?

The word 'claim' is used to describe two different types of request, which are more appropriately described as:

1. an application for reimbursement of direct loss, expense and/or damages arising from a clause in the contract that creates such an entitlement; or
2. a claim for damages arising from a breach, or a series of breaches, of the contract conditions.

The two different types of claim are often inextricably linked.

Reasons for claims

Unfortunately, understanding *how* claims arise does not necessarily provide a complete understanding of *why* claims arise. Legitimate claims are raised where there are breaches of contract and/or entitlements under the contract but there are a number of other reasons why spurious claims may be forwarded to their employers by contractors and subcontractors. Certifiers, including architects, project managers and engineers, clearly must understand the intent and merit of such claims to be able to classify them as spurious.

There are three main reasons for the submission of claims that are later shown to be unfounded or invalid.

The first is arguably the most common. There are genuine grounds for a claim of one type or another but, unfortunately, adequate contemporaneous records have not been kept. In these circumstances it is not unusual to find that contractors have acted on oral instructions or even on their own initiative, believing this course of action to be in the best interests of the project. Alternatively, they may have been issued with properly documented instructions or granted extensions of time but have failed to keep records of the resulting losses. In either case, the claim will be evidentially weak and the claimant may have to resort to submitting an unparticularised, global or rolled-up claim. Such claims are considered in detail in Section 4.

The second reason for an apparently spurious claim is that the contractor has genuinely incurred a loss on the project and wishes to have that loss made good, thus re-establishing the profitable position that was undoubtedly the contractor's impression of the situation at the outset. In many instances the contractor cannot be certain why these losses have arisen, but will be quite certain that they did not cause them. Unfortunately for contractors, there are many examples of how a loss could very easily be laid at their door, including inadequate tender provisions, low site productivity, poor supervision, inadequate supply of labour and materials and the effect of price escalation on labour, materials and subcontracts. Unless contractors can properly demonstrate that losses have arisen due to the acts or omissions of the employer, the case must fail.

The third reason for the submission of a speculative claim by a contractor is, quite simply, opportunism. In some instances an architect or employer's representative is perceived as being weak and, as a result, a strong contractor may see an opportunity to pressurise them into being too permissive in the granting of instructions and extensions of time. On other occasions the public purse is seen as a well from which extra cash can be drawn at will. Wily contractors may also perceive that some public and private concerns are so sensitive to public opinion that they will compromise and pay unmeritorious claims in order to avoid any adverse media coverage.

In each case where the claim is unfounded, the claimant intends to improve a financial position beyond that which is contractually and legally supported.

Impartiality and independence

The determination to increase profitability is not confined to contracting organisations. Employers may subject the architect or the supervising officer to intense pressure, encouraging them to reduce payments or refuse extensions of time. Architects, annoyed at such improper tactics, may act on their conscience and in strict accordance with the law, only to find that an errant employer is slow to honour their certificates, and is generally obstructive in regard to any attempt to administer the contract properly. It is not unknown for employers and contractors to starve financially weak companies of cash flow deliberately, in the hope that these companies will be in no position to fight for their proper entitlements later. Sadly, these tactics occasionally do succeed, but they also create disruptive and expensive conflict.

For almost two years I have been working as the expert witness on a dispute arising from a large project in the Middle East where the employer allegedly pressurised the engineer to under-certify. In addition, even the allegedly artificially low certified values were not paid in full. An international arbitration is now under way with both parties seeking to value the loss that the contractor has incurred, which is thought to be in excess of $500 million. The costs of this complex international action will probably exceed $10 million.

Cost of conflict

This raises another crucial point, namely that conflict in the construction industry is always costly and the need to resolve it diverts vital project management effort away from the successful completion of the project. A serious conflict can easily add 20 per cent or more to a project's final cost.

"conflict in the construction industry is always costly"

Self-evidently, absolute honesty in making claims and in responding to them will do much to reduce the potential for conflict. Some conflict in the prosecution and defence of a claim is inevitable because of hostile personalities, incompatible goals and different interpretations of the contract wording, but most conflict can be alleviated by adopting a polite, respectful and even-handed approach to the differences between the parties. A greater use of partnering, both pre-contract and during the currency of a contract, can also reduce conflict, as can the use of 'term contracting', where both parties have made a significant investment in their ongoing relationship.

Claims avoidance

As a practising expert witness I can say that 80 per cent of the claims I am instructed to value became inevitable before any work commenced on site. The majority of claims arise from poor procurement and pre-contract management. The main culprits are:

- proceeding on a design that is incomplete or which will need significant change
- tendering too early in the design process
- making a poor choice of tenderers and/or poor selection of successful bidder
- using an inappropriate standard form of contract, unfair bespoke contract or ill-advised amendments to the standard form of contract
- refusing to implement or comply with design freeze dates
- refusing to allow a reasonable time for completion.

Late design and late changes in design may cause contractors to work unproductively, stop work or demolish and rebuild completed works, all of which are extremely expensive. In some cases it is more economical to allow contractors to complete the contract works as planned and retrofit the changes later on a fixed price quotation.

Tendering too early and choosing the wrong contractor will result in shrewd contractors exploiting changes in order to enhance profitability. As a quantum expert witness on the British Library, I discovered that the contractor responsible for the hard landscaping had priced brickwork and paving at extremely high rates because the small quantities shown on the unfinished drawings would not skew his price. Predictably, there were huge increases in the amount of brickwork and paving installed, which netted the contractor margins in excess of 100 per cent.

Claims, particularly for breach of contract, are more likely to arise when the balance of benefits and burdens in a contract is tilted in favour of one party. Initially, contractors will accept the turnover but they will then seek to redress the balance by way of claims. They will often be assisted in the promulgation of their claims by the poor drafting of amendments to standard form contracts or of bespoke contracts. Writing and amending contracts is work for talented and brave lawyers, and for them only.

Finally on this list, there is no value in setting a time for completion that is not readily achievable. Again, contractors will accept an unrealistic time constraint to obtain the turnover, but will record every delay, disturbance and change, often ascribing to them unlikely periods of delay and thus requesting an unreasonable extension of time.

The Olympic Park offers some good examples of claims-avoidance techniques being implemented from the outset. In the early days of the project, many professionals were pressing for the stadia to be procured on NEC 3 Option C, Target

Cost with Activity Schedule and with realistic completion dates. We now know that most of those projects finished ahead of time and ahead of budget.

The key reasons for this success, in my opinion, were a fair balance of contractual burdens, early completion of design along with a design freeze, reluctance to introduce change, tight administrative control, realistic time scales for completion, valuation of changes as the work proceeded and the prompt resolution of disputes in two-party discussions as the works proceeded.

SUMMARY

Avoidable claims will continue to arise due to poor procurement procedures, and unforeseeable claims will arise due to the complexity and longevity of our projects.

These claims will be submitted in response to contractual or extra-contractual events and they may be legitimate or spurious.

However they arise, and regardless of which category they fall into, claims must be taken seriously and must be properly administered if we are to avoid the unnecessary escalation of disputes. This guide endeavours to explain, simply, how this can be done efficiently to protect the architect/certifier from criticism and/or legal action.

Section 2
Getting your certification right

In this Section:

- *Certifiers must be impartial and independent*
- *Certifier's obligations to follow the contract*
- *Payment under JCT Standard Building Contract with Quantities 2011 (JCT 2011 SBC/Q)*
- *Certifier's obligations to address loss and expense impartially*
- *Architect as quasi-arbitrator?*
- *Liability to the employer*
- *Liability to the contractor*

Certifiers must be impartial and independent

A certifier must be impartial and independent, if they are to carry out their duties properly. As long ago as 1993, Sir Michael Latham noted in his landmark Interim Report on the future of the construction industry, *Trust and Money*, that the architectural profession takes the view that the JCT contracts are specifically drafted in terms which lay the professional duty of *impartial* contract administration upon the architect.

Obviously many things have changed since the 1990s but, even now, traditional building and civil engineering contracts of the JCT, NEC, ICE and FIDIC types are drafted in terms that allow the employer to engage the contractor to carry out the works in the knowledge that the contract administrator will act impartially.

The history of claims in arbitration and in the courts bears testimony to the principle that a project based on an agreement which presupposes that the contract administrator will act impartially and independently of the employer will only be a timely and economic success if the contract administrator acts fairly.

While not a party to the main contract, the architect, engineer or project manager usually oversees all aspects of contract administration, including the valuation of measured work and variations, ascertainment of the contractor's entitlement to loss and expense (however described) and the assessment of extensions of time. If those individuals do not exercise their powers with impartiality, or in accordance with the contract, disputes will arise and loss and expense will be claimed.

Certifier's obligations to follow the contract

The architect or contract administrator will have entered into some form of agreement with the employer which carried the obligation to safeguard the interests of the employer. This means that appropriate selection of, and adherence to, the contract is crucial. Once the contract form has been agreed and the works have commenced, architects can be too permissive, for instance, by allowing inappropriate extensions of time, or they can be too restrictive, such as not allowing time or money as the contract dictates they should. Every failure to comply with the contract and safeguard the employer is likely to bring conflict and provoke a potential argument over the value of the loss and expense the contractor has incurred.

It is vital, therefore, that the architect or contract administrator implements the contract conditions with precision to avoid problems. Unfortunately, since the introduction of the Housing Grants, Construction and Regeneration Act 1996 (sometimes referred to as the Construction Act 1996), one of the main causes of dispute has been the late or incorrect issue of payment certificates, a problem that will become more prevalent unless everyone is prepared to familiarise themselves with the current construction acts and their impact on the main contract forms. To avoid any doubt as to the impact of the Act, I have summarised the provisions below. Throughout this book I will be referencing the JCT Standard Building Contract with Quantities 2011 when referring to JCT 2011.

Payment under JCT Standard Building Contract with Quantities 2011 (JCT 2011 SBC/Q)

The JCT forms, amended to comply with the Housing Grants, Construction and Regeneration Act 1996, Part II, Construction Contracts and the Local Democracy,

Economic Development and Construction Act 2009, section 8, Construction Contracts, give clear instructions to architects on how to produce interim certificates. Any failure to follow the rules is likely to result in loss to the contractor and, potentially, the employer.

"Any failure to follow the rules is likely to result in loss to the contractor and, potentially, the employer"

Architects are under considerable pressure to ensure that interim certificates are issued in a timely fashion and with proper explanation. Not to do so leaves the way open for contractors to recover the sums they believe are due. This in turn may lead to a dispute or, if it occurs late in the project, it may lead to overpayment and may require a subsequent arbitration to recover monies not due but paid under the contract. The payment process that allows this to happen is incorporated into the JCT forms as a result of the above named legislation. In short, the provisions are as follows:

- The due dates for interim payments by the employer are stated in the contract particulars (see clause 4.9.1).
- The architect shall, no later than five days after the due date, issue an interim certificate stating the sum they believe is due and the basis of calculation (see clause 4.10.1).
- The contractor may make interim applications to the quantity surveyor no later than seven days before the due date, setting out the amount they consider to be due and the basis of their calculation (see clause 4.11.1).
- If the architect fails to issue an interim certificate then the contractor can rely on the interim application value as the interim payment notice (see clause 4.11.2.1).
- Alternatively, if the contractor has not made an interim application they can give an interim payment notice explaining how much they consider to be due and why (see clause 4.11.2.2).
- Unless a valid pay less notice has been issued (clause 4.12.5) then, within 14 days after the due date, the interim certificate value or the interim payment notice value (if no interim certificate has been issued) must be paid by the employer (see clause 4.12.1).

It would be surprising if a failure to pay as stipulated above did not lead to some form of partial suspension, total suspension and/or to an adjudication; all are allowed under the above Acts. It is vital, therefore, for architects to comply with the provisions of the Act, as integrated into the new forms of contract, because every suspension or partial suspension will give rise to claims for extensions of time and loss and expense.

Certifier's obligations to address loss and expense impartially

Under the JCT standard form of contract, the architect or contract administrator, appointed by the employer, either ascertains loss and expense and carries out valuations, or delegates these responsibilities to the quantity surveyor. Delegation of these matters to others has been common practice for decades and is anticipated by those drafting the JCT forms of contract.

Under NEC 3 this certifying role falls to the project manager who notifies of and assesses compensation events under core clauses 61 and 63 respectively. In FIDIC the process is contained in contractor's claims clause 20.1, where the engineer is expected to make a fair determination.

> *"to what extent can the architect be genuinely impartial and administer the contract fairly? "*

Given that the architect or engineer is contracted to the employer but has no contractual link to the contractor, the question inevitably arises: to what extent can the architect be genuinely impartial and administer the contract fairly?

In arbitration and litigation submissions claimants have often argued that architectural practices with a small client base could not afford to offend their paymasters and so did their bidding. This accusation of partiality becomes even more of an issue on engineering projects when a bespoke, or heavily amended, contract names a member of the employer's staff as the engineer or engineer's representative, which is not uncommon.

Architect as quasi-arbitrator

In the late 19th and early 20th centuries the courts held that an architect or engineer held sway between the parties as an arbitrator or quasi-arbitrator (*Jackson v. Barry Railway Company* (1893)). This unfortunate choice of words created the false impression that an architect's or engineer's role was somehow judicial as opposed to merely administrative. This is a fallacy that we still hear repeated 120 years later.

In the many cases since 1893 the courts have repeatedly confirmed that while engineers and architects have the primary duties of honesty and impartiality, they have no judicial or quasi-judicial powers. The courts have noted, however, that an architect, although the agent of the employer, frequently has to adjudicate upon matters for which the architect was partly responsible. Thus, the courts believe it is imperative that architects and engineers are able to maintain a fair and judicial view of the rights of the parties.

Liability to the employer

The House of Lords held in *Sutcliffe v. Thackrah and Others* (1974) that an architect, in certifying, was acting not as an arbitrator or quasi-arbitrator but as the agent of the employer. As such, he was liable to the employer for negligent certification. To quote from the helpful judgment of Lord Reid:

> *the architect has two different types of function to perform. In many matters he is bound to act on his client's instructions, whether he agrees with them or not; but in many other matters requiring professional skill he must form and act on his own opinion.*

> *The building owner and the contractor make their contract on the understanding that in all such matters (e.g. where he has to value work, or approve it) the architect will act in a fair and unbiased manner and it must therefore be implicit in the owner's contract with the architect that he shall not only exercise due care and skill but also reach such decisions fairly holding the balance between his client and the contractor.*

The architect's duty has been discussed in other modern cases, in *London Borough of Merton v. Stanley Hugh Leach Ltd* (1985), Vinelott J. defined the role of the architect in the following terms: 'The Building Owner … undertakes that although the Architect may be engaged or employed by him, he will leave him free to exercise his discretions fairly and without improper interference.'

So, the law suggests that the architect is not a quasi-judge or arbitrator but has a duty to exercise discretions fairly. The courts are also keen to point out that the employer must not interfere with the architect's independence as such interference may constitute a breach of contract.

Liability to the contractor

What is more difficult to assess is the architect's potential liability to the contractor if the architect fails properly to discharge their duties. It might seem reasonable to assume that it is only fair that the architect should have a duty to the contractor to exercise reasonable skill and care when issuing payment certificates (including any ascertainment of loss and expense) or granting extensions of time, and there is certainly some case law to support this proposition.

Most pertinent is the decision in *Michael Salliss & Co. Ltd v. Carlil and William F. Newman & Associates* (1987), where the Official Referee, Judge Fox-Andrews, concluded that a contractor had a right to recover damages against an unfair architect:

> *If the architect unfairly promotes the building employer's interest by low certification or merely fails properly to exercise reasonable care and skill in his certification it is reasonable that the contractor should not only have the right as against the owner to have the certificate reviewed in arbitration but should also have the right to recover damages against the unfair architect.*

This simple restatement of the prevailing law was unfortunately thrown into confusion by the decision of the Court of Appeal in *Pacific Associates Inc. and Another v. Baxter and Others* (1988). In that case the court held that a disclaimer in the head contract and the presence of an arbitration clause prevented a contractor from succeeding against an under-certifying engineer.

That case has not found many admirers and people often prefer the judgment in *Davy Offshore Ltd v. Emerald Field Contracting Ltd* (1991). In the words of the Official Referee, Judge Thayne Forbes:

> *In my judgment, it is clear that the obligation to act fairly is concerned with those duties of the architect/engineer which require him to use his professional judgment in holding the balance between his client and the contractor. Such duties are those where the architect/engineer is obliged to make a decision or form an opinion which affects the rights of the parties to the contract, for example, valuations of work, ascertaining direct loss and expense, granting extensions of time, etc. When making such decisions pursuant to his duties under the contract, the architect/engineer is obliged to act fairly.*

So, the law suggests that, for the architect or engineer to be liable to the contractor (with whom ordinarily they have no contract), the principles establishing the legal doctrine of tort must be satisfied. In essence, if the architect is negligent in their actions and causes loss or physical harm to befall the contractor, they should compensate the contractor.

The law of torts and particularly the law relating to pure economic loss in construction cases is complex and beyond the scope of this text. Any reader who wishes to delve more deeply into the topic should read the latest editions of *Hudson's Building and Engineering Contracts* and *Keating on Construction Contracts*, both of which deal with the issues in detail. For those who have no wish to delve into those worthy tomes I summarise their comments on architects' and engineers' liabilities in the following summary.

SUMMARY

The architect or contract administrator who does not certify in accordance with the law and the contract will face adjudications and/or claims for loss and expense for breach.

Further, the learned commentators suggest that:

- it is possible that an architect or engineer could be found to be liable to the contractor for negligent certification, particularly if there were no arbitration clause that allowed the contractor to remedy the under-certification.

Unfortunately, this statement does not help as most contracts, even bespoke contracts, do contain an arbitration clause.

Perhaps more helpfully they note, premised upon the comments of May L.J. in *John Mowlem v. Eagle Star Insurance* (1992), that:

- it is more likely that an architect could be pursued for the tort of procuring a breach of contract if they deliberately misapplied the contract terms with the intention of depriving the contractor of sums to which they would otherwise be entitled.

So, certifiers who fulfil their contractual obligations and act independently and fairly have little need to worry about being pursued by either the employer or the contractor.

Section 3
Receiving a claim

In this Section:

- *Claims under the contract*
- *Claims for breach of contract*
- *Intermingled claims*

Claims under the contract

The standard JCT building contracts, along with many other standard forms, enable contractors, on their compliance with certain prescribed procedures, to be reimbursed under the contract for the time and money consequences of delay and disruption. However, as the *RIBA Good Practice Guide: Extensions of Time* (2008) deals with the recovery of time in great detail, I will restrict my commentary to money claims.

The standard form contracts usually define the circumstances in which money claims can be made by the contractor, an example of this being the wording of JCT 2011 Standard Building Contract with Quantities (SBC/Q) Clauses 4.23 to 4.26 which refer to 'loss and/or expense'.

The term 'loss and/or expense' may reasonably be described as covering:

- monies lost which ought to have been received
- expenditure of money which ought not to have been required.

Later in this section we will see that both of these heads of claim might equally be recoverable under the common law, which attempts to put the claimant back into the position they enjoyed prior to any breach, insofar as that can be achieved by financial compensation.

Under clause 4.23 of JCT 2011 a contractor is able, under the terms of the contract, to recover direct loss and/or expense where the progress of the works has been materially affected by certain specified matters. These are set out in JCT 2011, clause 4.24 as 'relevant matters':

4.24.1   Variations (excluding those where loss and/or expense is included in the Confirmed Acceptance of a Variation Quotation but including any other matters or instructions which under these Conditions are to be treated as, or as requiring, a Variation);

4.24.2   Architect/Contract Administrator's instructions:

.1   under clause 3.15 or 3.16 (excluding an instruction for expenditure of a Provisional Sum for defined work);

.2   for the opening up for inspection or testing of any work, materials or goods under clause 3.17 (including making good), unless the cost is provided for in the Contract Bills or unless the inspection or test shows that the work, materials or goods are not in accordance with this Contract;

.3   in relation to any discrepancy or divergence referred to in clause 2.15;

4.24.3   compliance with clause 3·22·1 or with Architect/Contract Administrator's instructions under clause 3·22·2;

4.24.4   the execution of work for which an Approximate Quantity is not a reasonably accurate forecast of the quantity of work required;

4.24.5   any impediment, prevention or default, whether by act or omission, by the Employer, the Architect/Contract Administrator, the Quantity Surveyor or any of the Employer's Persons, except to the extent caused or contributed to by any default, whether by act or omission, of the Contractor or of any of the Contractor's Persons.

"contractors should make every effort to rely upon the contract terms rather than the general law"

There are sound financial reasons why contractors should make every effort to rely upon the contract terms rather than the general law:

- the ascertainment will be usually made by a quantity surveyor familiar with the works and with the claimant

- any ascertainment will be paid as the works proceed, assisting cash flow
- there is little formality required in presentation, saving costs
- there is no requirement for expensive consultants or lawyers
- ascertainment can still be challenged in accordance with the contractual rules for dispute resolution.

In short, most practitioners would recommend utilising the contractual claims mechanism wherever it is possible to do so.

Having explained how contractual claims arise, and the benefits gained from making any claim for reimbursement under the contract, the subject will be examined further in later sections. In Section 5: *Valuing contract claims and breaches of contract*, the issue of how such claims are analysed, how they are proved and how they are quantified is addressed.

Claims for breach of contract

As noted in Section 1: *Basic principles*, the contract forms will never be able to anticipate every event capable of arising on a complex, prototype building constructed over a long period of time. As a result, contractors will encounter difficulties that are not listed as 'relevant matters'. In such cases there are two options:

1. the parties agree to amend the contract between them to manage and/or resolve the issue, or
2. they do nothing and await a claim that the contract has been breached.

The wording in clause 4.24, as quoted above, is very broad in its interpretation and it obviously seeks to encompass every possible failure of the employer and their team, but we can still expect to see breaches being alleged. With the cooperation of the contractor, many of the issues that would have been absolute breaches under older versions of the JCT forms could now be said to be covered by the catch-all clause 4.24.

Examples of past breaches that have exercised people sufficiently to send them to court include architects refusing to change the completion date, architects refusing to certify appropriately and architects instructing acceleration measures when there exists no contractual mechanism or right to do so.

An employer, seeking to avoid third party intervention, may argue that these issues fall to be ascertained under the broad wording of JCT 2011, clause 4.24.

If, for any reason, a contractor is successful in proving that a failure is not covered by the contractual machinery then it stands to be considered under the general law.

Because legal precedent suggests that the term 'loss and/or expense' is to be interpreted in accordance with the principles for the recovery of damages at common law, there can only be limited differences between the methods of evaluation of the two types of claim. Both types of claim will be constrained by the rule in *Hadley v. Baxendale* (1854), which is described as having two 'limbs':

1. damages arising naturally from the breach, and
2. damages dependent upon special circumstances.

Lawyers would argue that what is recoverable under the first limb is the financial loss which directly and naturally results in the ordinary course of events. In JCT terms this would include any financial loss arising from any of the clause 4.24 matters, such matters being capable of ascertainment under the contract rules.

The second limb will include damages that were foreseeable by the parties, given their special knowledge of the project, the parties and their commercial arrangements at the time of contracting. This may well include consequential damages, financing and interest. Many employers would be perfectly content for their quantity surveyors to address the issue of financing in their ascertainment under the heading loss and/or expense. Likewise, in reviewing common law claims, many employers would consider that a claim for ordinary financing or interest rates – that is, contemporary market rates of interest – would fall under the first limb of *Hadley v. Baxendale* because in the real world money is never free. Obviously, if a contractor has some onerous overdraft arrangements with a punishing rate of interest that may fall under the second limb, special circumstances, it would be wise to make that arrangement known to the employer at the time of contracting to ensure full recompense.

There are textbooks that devote many thousands of words to the topic of what is included in the second limb of *Hadley v. Baxendale* and the thorny subject of financing costs and so, once again, I would refer an enthusiast to the latest editions of *Hudson's* or *Keating* as noted earlier in this text.

Intermingled claims

There has been much legal commentary, and not a few court cases, on the issue of pursuing claims under the contract and extra contractual claims separately. The sensible approach now adopted by the courts and arbitrators is nicely expressed by Vinelot J. in *London Borough of Merton v. Stanley Hugh Leach Ltd* (1985):

> *[The contractor] may prefer to wait until completion of the work and join the claim for damages for breach of the obligation to provide instructions, drawings and the like in good time with other claims for damages for breach of obligations under the contract.*

His statement was made in the context of contractor's right to bring a common law damages claim under JCT 63, which was less inclusive than the current clause 4.24 in JCT 2011, but his words still resonate with courts and tribunals today. As a practising expert witness who appears before the courts and international tribunals, I can say that there has been no successful objection to the presentation of mixed claims in the 20 years I have been working in this arena.

So, how might such an occurrence arise? In what circumstances might we face a mixed claim?

In the early years of this century I was appointed as the delay and quantum expert witness on a troubled project at Heathrow Airport. The bespoke contract contained all of the 'relevant events' that were present in the then current JCT forms. The facts were broadly as listed below:

a. *The contractor alleged late possession of the site.*
b. *The contractor alleged that significant changes were made after installation had taken place.*
c. *The contractor alleged late delivery of drawings and other information.*
d. *Instructions and variations were issued and inferred.*
e. *Extensions of time were not granted because the operational date was said to be immovable; acceleration was demanded.*
f. *The contractor's employment was terminated.*

While *b*, *c* and *d* fell to be addressed under the contract conditions, *a* and *e* did not fall under any relevant event. The termination could have been addressed under the contract conditions but the contractor challenged the contractual right to terminate, given the circumstances that prevailed at termination.

Despite a determined effort to reduce the matters to be laid before the court for settlement, the variations were not ascertained and the whole matter was litigated, at huge expense.

It is always in everyone's interests to agree what can be agreed, especially if that involves an ascertainment over which the quantity surveyor has full control.

SUMMARY

Claims can be made under the contract clauses, as extra contractual claims or as a mixture of contractual claims and common law claims.

Sections 4 and 5 will revisit these different types of claim to provide an understanding of the level of evidence that is required from a claimant if they are to be successful in establishing liability and recovering their money losses.

Before moving on, however, it is worth repeating that every reasonable effort should be made to permit claims to fall under the contract terms so that they can be ascertained under the control of the architect and quantity surveyor. Once a third party resolution is under way the outcome is unpredictable.

Section 4
Establishing liability

In this Section:

- *Liability generally*
- *Existence of an obligation*
- *Breach of an obligation*
- *Resultant financial damage*
- *Cause and effect*
- *Global claims*

Liability generally

Whenever a claimant seeks a remedy at law, whether in arbitration or litigation, they are obliged to set out the particulars of their case, in order to clearly establish who they think is liable and why. At one time a claimant could commence proceedings with a very general complaint and build their pleading as the case progressed. This obviously wasted a good deal of court time and incurred a great deal of cost to both claimant and defendant. This is no longer acceptable. Judges will examine the pleadings in great detail before allowing the case to go forward. Judges have been known to demand the outcome of the programming report before allowing the case to proceed to timetabling. Some arbitral panels will follow this lead but many will still proceed on inadequate particularisation.

It is important for contract administrators, quantity surveyors and employers to understand the level of particularisation that tribunals require so as not to be too permissive or, worse, too restrictive.

The claimant must particularise their claim sufficiently to allow the respondent properly to understand the case they are to answer. To satisfy the legal obligations the claimant must provide the respondent with sufficient detail in the Points of Claim to enable the respondent to defend their position. It is for the claimant to show that they have been wronged, that the wrongdoing caused them damage and that the damage resulted in the claimant suffering a direct loss. The claimant is then expected to prove the financial implications of that damage by using reasonable calculations.

"full particularisation will usually assist the process of negotiating an appropriate settlement"

It should be noted that full particularisation will usually assist the process of negotiating an appropriate settlement, thus avoiding the expense of third party settlement.

Existence of an obligation

For the purposes of contractual claims, as opposed to those in negligence, the claimant must first show that there is a legally binding contract between the parties, creating rights and obligations. It is then for the claimant to show that, incorporated into that contract, either expressly or impliedly, are terms and conditions that give rise to an obligation or duty on the part of the respondent which has been breached. The construction industry is notorious for either completing the contract agreement late or never completing the agreement at all. Many cases reaching the courts have as their first issues the questions:

- Was there an agreement on the contract terms?
- If so, what terms are incorporated into the agreement?
- If there is no contract in existence, on what basis is the contractor to be reimbursed?

It is unfortunate that judicial intervention is so often needed on so fundamental an issue. Where a standard form of contract is the basis of the parties' agreement, then the relevant duties and obligations are those set out in the clauses of the relevant standard form as added to by common law implied terms.

Breach of an obligation

Having established that the respondent has certain defined obligations to the claimant under the terms of the contract, the claimant must show which of these obligations have been breached. It is also necessary to show when and how they were breached; a simple accusation is insufficient. This step is vital both for breaches which have an agreed procedure for their resolution within the contract clauses and breaches which, in the absence of agreement, have to be remedied by a court or arbitrator.

Resultant financial damage

Once it has been established that an obligation has been breached, the claimant must
show that some financial loss has been
incurred. The major exception to this rule is
pre-agreed, or liquidated and ascertained,

"the claimant must show that some financial loss has been incurred"

damages. In the case of such damages, the parties agree beforehand the conse-
quence of a breach and impose the financial remedy without further assessment
or proof of loss being necessary once the 'trigger' event has occurred.

If the damages are not agreed in advance, then the damage must be proved, but
this is not as simple as it might sound. There are three possible reasons for this
difficulty:

- A financial loss has not been incurred.
- A financial loss has been incurred but cannot be evidenced.
- A financial loss has been incurred but cannot be connected to the breach.

First, claimants may have suffered because of a breach of an obligation. They
have been inconvenienced, worked harder, worked longer, perhaps they have
changed their established method of operation. But, when they come to examine
the damage, they find that they have still completed within budget, or within the
contract price. A financial loss has not been incurred. Their sterling efforts have
prevented a financial loss arising. In such circumstances they feel as if they should
be rewarded, but there will be no cause of action without a financial loss.

In a case where I was the quantum expert, I discovered that the employer's
efforts to make dwellings available to the contractor for refitting, as agreed, were
thwarted by uncooperative tenants. The plumbers, electricians and heating engineers were obliged to work whenever they could gain access, often traversing the
whole length of the housing estate many times in a day. This was a clear breach of
obligation for which a claim could be made. While researching the claim I forensi-
cally examined the contractor's accounts and discovered that, despite the problems affecting all of the operatives, they were all being paid on a piecework basis
and not according to hours spent. Thus, when they finished a dwelling they were

paid exactly the contracted amount of £2,000. The contractor had not suffered a financial loss and the case collapsed.

Second, contractors are notoriously poor record keepers and in many cases they have undoubtedly made a financial loss but cannot prove it. Sometimes they attempt to rely on suppliers' and subcontractors' records which are incomplete. On other occasions the losses arising from the breach are so intermingled with contract costs that they cannot be separated; unless they can be, the claim will fail.

Third, the contractor can prove a financial loss but cannot provide evidence to show that it arose from the breach, a situation referred to as 'cause and effect', discussed next.

"The sole reason for a claimant seeking a financial remedy, is either to recover losses or to avoid financial penalties"

The sole reason for a claimant seeking a financial remedy under the contract, or damages from a court or arbitrator, is either to recover losses or to avoid financial penalties. The claimant's obligation was neatly described by Asquith L.J. in *Victoria Laundry (Windsor) Ltd v. Newman Industries Ltd* (1949):

> It is well settled that the governing purpose of damages is to put the party whose rights have been violated in the same position, so far as money can do, as if his rights had been observed.

Some claimants will seek to improve their situation or to secure a bonus for their efforts, but this is not the intention of the standard form contracts or of the common law.

Cause and effect

Once we have established that there was an obligation which was breached and that financial damage arose, we have to establish that the loss and the breach are linked. It is for the claimant to prove, on the balance of probabilities, that the loss incurred arose directly as a result of the breach.

As noted above, not all breaches cause financial damage, though it is often asserted by claimants that *every* breach causes financial damage. Architects and other contract administrators should ensure that this linkage is not overlooked when assessing claims, as it is common practice for claims practitioners to leap straight from proving a breach to attaching a loss to it. In practice, while some breaches will be easily linked to a loss, others will be almost impossible to link. One example of this is illustrated by a case study carried out on a central London office block some years ago.

After the contract for the office block was signed and the working hours agreed upon (6 a.m. to 6 p.m.), the local authority placed an embargo on deliveries before 9.30 a.m. because the site entrance was on an important arterial route. Most deliveries could be rescheduled with no financial loss, but concrete could not be delivered and pumped until around 10 a.m. This was a huge blow to a contractor building a reinforced concrete structure using slip-forming methodology. As a result, the contractor wisely recorded all costs, losses and delays and thus the nexus or link was established.

- Obligation of the employer: provide access at 6 a.m.
- Breach: no access until 9.30 a.m.
- Financial loss: overtime working, part-time operatives on site in peak times, costs of delay.
- Cause and effect: measured losses arose entirely due to limited working hours.

The result was a neatly packaged claim evidencing cause and effect which was settled quickly.

On the same project, the mechanical and electrical (M&E) contractor had contracted to use the tower crane to lift their materials to each floor. Unfortunately, the employer was obliged to remove the tower crane early, after complaints from a neighbour were upheld. Most M&E equipment had to be taken up in a shared service lift or up stairs. Here again there was a clear obligation, a breach of that obligation and even a clear loss, but when the financial loss claim was tested no one could say with any certainty that the additional hours claimed were actually incurred as a result of the disrupted working practices. All that was needed was a system of allocation sheets which stated 'hand carrying materials', accurately priced, and the nexus would have been made and the claim would have succeeded.

Global claims

By following the steps outlined above the necessary linkage between cause and effect can usually be established. However, failure to demonstrate this linkage can be fatal to a claim, given the very strict rules which apply to the presentation of pleadings for use in arbitration and litigation. In *Wharf Properties Ltd and Another v. Eric Cumine Associates (No. 2)* (1991) Lord Oliver stated that compliance with Order 18 of the Rules of the Supreme Court, which defines the method of setting out legal pleadings, required:

> *a plaintiff to plead his case with such particularity as is sufficient to alert the opposite party to the case which is going to be made against him at the trial … The failure even to attempt to specify any discernible nexus between the wrong alleged and the consequent delay provides, to use [Counsel's] phrase, 'no agenda' for the trial.*

Global claims, also known as rolled-up and total loss claims, frequently fail to establish this nexus. Often, no attempt is made to find a link and the global claim becomes a lazy claimant's way of seeking reimbursement.

While a global claim which makes no effort to establish cause and effect is likely to fail, there is hope for claimants who have provided at least some evidence. The courts have made allowances in the past when, despite every effort of the claimant, some losses could not be directly linked to their causes. The cases of *J. Crosby and Sons Ltd v. Portland Urban District Council* (1967) and the *London Borough of Merton v. Stanley Hugh Leach Ltd* (1985) involved the judge's or arbitrator's right to award a wrap-up sum in regard to particular heads of claim, which were dependent on a complex interaction between the consequences of a number of events. Despite these intricacies, which made accurate apportionment difficult, the cases were upheld.

Thus, if a contractor can link the majority of their losses to individual causes, and if they can prove an outstanding financial loss, the tribunal might be of a mind to allow some monies if it is convinced that the losses arose from a complex interaction of events which cannot be separated.

"failure to specify the factual consequences of alleged breaches is usually at the heart of a global claim"

In essence, what Lord Oliver did in *Wharf Properties* was to distinguish these cases from *Wharf Properties*, reminding claimants that it remains their duty to plead their case with such particularity as is necessary to alert the opposite party to the case that must be answered at trial. On the face of the pleadings in *Wharf Properties* there was no real attempt to specify the factual consequences of alleged breaches of contract. The failure to specify the factual consequences of alleged breaches is usually at the heart of a global claim.

The simplest form of global claim is represented by the naive formula:

- Total costs incurred by the claimant: £1,000,000
- Less: recovery on contract value and variations: £800,000
- Claim for loss and expense: **£200,000**

Global claims may be dressed up in many different ways but, when properly analysed, they will all fail to identify each and every event and establish the nexus between each event and the financial loss.

A global claim will usually be presented in one of three ways.

1. It may assert that there is no contract, or that the contract terms are invalid for want of proper incorporation. The claim will then suggest that the court or arbitrator should allow a reasonable price for the work done. This is often referred to by lawyers as a *quantum meruit* assessment, the value the work merits.

2. Another approach sometimes taken is that, on realising that the contract is unlikely to be swept away by the tribunal, the claimant will instead seek to base their claim on vague allegations of the respondent's failures or other deficiencies. The claimant may then list a variety of allegations, often poorly particularised, some of which are valid and some clearly invalid. While they make no effort to properly link cause with effect, it is hoped that a judge or arbitrator will see the list and, believing that there is no smoke without fire, make a favourable award.

3. The most common approach is to be specific and precise in proving the breaches, provide masses of evidence in support of the allegations, but then to submit an unparticularised financial claim that fails to identify which allegation caused which loss. Claims consultants usually cite case law to justify this approach and often rely on the case of *J. Crosby and Sons Ltd v. Portland Urban District Council* (1967) which has been mentioned previously.

In *Crosby*, the arbitrator had made a supplemental award in respect of a number of items where money could not be specifically allocated because individual causes could not be identified. Donaldson J. confirmed, on appeal, that the arbitrator was empowered to make such an award. In upholding the award he said:

> *I can see no reason why he [the arbitrator] should not recognise the realities of the situation and make individual awards in respect of those parts of individual items of the claim which can be dealt with in isolation and a sup-plementary award in respect of the remainder of these claims as a composite whole.*

This approach was also adopted by Vinelott J. in *Merton v. Leach*, when he indi-cated that failure by a claimant to attempt to attribute a loss to a particular breach was unacceptable:

> *a rolled-up award can only be made in a case where the loss or expense attributable to each head of claim cannot really strictly be separated ... and where apart from that practical impossibility the conditions which have to be satisfied before the award can be made have been satisfied in relation to each head of claim.*

In the case of *Mid Glamorgan County Council v. J. Devonald Williams & Partner* (1992), Mr Recorder Tackaberry QC, sitting as an Official Referee on the defend-ants' application to strike out the plaintiff's claim because of an alleged lack of particularisation, reviewed the existing case law before he suggested the follow-ing guidelines:

> (i) *Where delay or damage is proved and all of the conditions applicable to every such event have been satisfied, but it is impossible for the plaintiff to divide the financial loss between the various heads of claim, then the plaintiff may still succeed.*

> (ii) *Where there has been delay or damage but the plaintiff cannot show or does not try to show precisely what caused each event and how it affected the outcome for each event, then he will probably fail.*

> *If the claim falls under (ii) above, the plaintiff may fail to get to the hearing stage as the respondent may be granted a striking out order which would prevent the plaintiff from pursuing the claim in that particular format and perhaps at all.*

Further evidence that this viewpoint prevails in the legal community can be found in the learned texts on the subject. In his book *Construction Contracts: Principles and Cause and Effect Policies in Tort and Contract* (now out of print), I. N. Duncan Wallace QC points out that global or total loss claims often ignore the hours that are inevitably lost on every contract due to weather, labour shortages, poor supervision, bad site organisation and faulty estimating. In his view, if the claimant has only provided total loss evidence, namely that all losses arose as a result of the respondent's breaches,

"global or total loss claims often ignore the hours that are inevitably lost on every contract"

and the respondent can show that some of the losses are the claimant's fault, then a court or arbitrator will have an insurmountable difficulty in finding for the claimant to the extent that the claim may be rejected in its entirety.

However, in the recent Technology and Construction Court case of *Walter Lilly & Company v. Giles Patrick Cyril Mackay, DMW Developments Ltd* (2012), Mr Justice Akenhead provided a lengthy judgment which broadly followed the principles established in the earlier Scottish case of *John Doyle Construction Ltd v. Laing Management (Scotland) Ltd* (2002). In his judgment, Mr Justice Akenhead held that, if a claimant contractor were found to have been responsible for causing or contributing to the global loss, this would not necessarily mean that their global claim would fail. Instead, the amount for which the contractor is responsible would be deducted from the global loss. While this is a commendable approach, in practice it often fails because the contractor who makes a global claim usually has no records to assist the court in adjudging what proportion of the global loss was of the contractor's own making.

Confirming the continuing relevance of the earlier cases, Mr Justice Akenhead expressed the opinion that there would be no need for a court to go down the global or total cost route if the actual cost attributable to individual loss-causing events could be readily or practically determined.

Again referencing the earlier cases, he added that, while there is nothing wrong in principle with a total or global cost claim, there are added evidential difficulties which a claimant contractor will have to overcome. For example, a claimant contractor will generally have to establish that the loss which they have incurred would not have been incurred in any event. This is a further reference to the necessary exclusion of the costs arising from the claimant contractor's own defaults or failings.

In the view of Mr Justice Akenhead, to bring a global claim, a claimant contractor does not have to show that it is impossible to plead and prove cause and effect in the normal way but rather, subject to contractual restrictions, the claimant simply has to prove their case on a balance of probabilities. That is, the claimant has to prove that the events occurred and that they caused delay and/or disruption, which in turn caused loss.

Even after considering the findings in the *Walter Lilly* case, it can be seen that very little has changed in the way that tribunals and judges view global claims.

SUMMARY

A fully evidenced claim that properly establishes cause and effect and reasonably quantifies the losses for each event will probably succeed.

Such a claim may also succeed on those items of quantification that are rolled up, provided the claimant has demonstrated that this method of claims presentation was only adopted because of the impossibility of completely disentangling a number of interlinking circumstances. In the words of Vinelott J. in *Merton* v *Leach*:

> *If application is made … for reimbursement of direct loss and/or expense attributable to more than one head of claim and at a time when the loss and expense comes to be ascertained it is impracticable to disentangle … the parts directly attributable to each head of claim, then provided of course that the contractor has not unreasonably delayed in making his claim and so has himself created the difficulty the Architect must ascertain the global loss directly attributable to the causes.*

Lord Oliver in *Wharf Properties*, Mr Recorder Tackaberry QC in *J. Devonald Williams* and I. N. Duncan Wallace in his learned textbook all make it clear that a claim which relies exclusively on global or total loss methodology and which does not seriously attempt to link cause and effect is likely to fail.

Finally, Mr Justice Akenhead has taken us a step further in our understanding by acknowledging that a global claim could potentially succeed if the claimant contractor can evidence and value their contribution to the overall loss and deduct it from the global claim.

Section 5
Valuing contract claims and breaches of contract

In this Section:

- *Final accounts*
- *Valuing prolongation*
- *Valuing head office contributions, use of formulae*
- *Loss of productivity and acceleration*
- *Valuing acceleration measures*
- *Valuing disruption*
- *Financing and interest*
- *Claim preparation costs*

Final accounts

Complex projects will almost inevitably produce complex financial accounts. Traditionally, any reimbursable costs incurred by the contractor are recovered by one of two methods: the final account or the loss and expense claim.

The final account should be simple enough to agree as it will contain only the following straightforward items:

- the contract price
- adjustments for extra or reduced works
- adjustment of prime cost and provisional sums
- evaluation of daywork

• evaluation of the consequences of price escalation on materials, plant and labour, sometimes called fluctuations.

However, nothing is entirely predictable and there are often disputes over some or all of these items. The main points of contention seem to arise from the evaluation of the extra work, the definition of daywork and the operation of the price escalation clauses. A brief review of each of these troublesome issues may help.

Variations

There is a large degree of similarity in the approach of the various standard form contracts to the valuation of additional or omitted work. These universal principles are:

1. where instructed work is of similar character, is executed in similar conditions and does not significantly change the quantity, then contract rates shall be used
2. where the work is of similar character but is not executed in similar conditions and/or the quantity differs, then the contract rates are to be adjusted to allow for the differences
3. where the work differs in character, then fair rates are applied.

In those cases where the instructed work is to be valued by measurement, using one of the three rules above, then the contractor will try to show that the characteristics of the work are different. This will leave the contractor free to use rates other than those used in competitive tendering and which are found in the contract documents. In many instances the contractor will have a sound argument. Where additional small quantities are ordered after the bulk materials have been ordered, the expected discounts are often lost. Plasterwork to curved surfaces may be more costly to carry out than the same plasterwork on flat surfaces.

The contractor may also find that the timing of the extra work causes disturbance to the progress of the works or that it may require the re-hire of plant that has been off-hired. The contractor is well advised to incorporate all such items, as well as additional preliminary costs and overheads, into the variation account. Experience has shown that variation costs are usually more readily certified by the employer's representative

"variation costs are usually more readily certified by the employer's representative than claim costs"

than claim costs. Those costs that are not recovered in the variation account, such as the disruption caused by variations, may find their way into a loss and expense claim.

Daywork

Where work is incapable of valuation by measurement, then the daywork rates incorporated into the contract are used to value the labour, plant and materials on a reimbursable basis.

Historically, architects and employers have been wary of contractors' use of daywork rates or other reimbursable rates. This is because in any reimbursable situation the whole risk of the operatives' time and cost is transferred to the employer, who has no control over the labour. The employer may reasonably believe that in such circumstances there is no incentive for the contractor to work efficiently.

The contract administrator does at least have the right to demand the daywork sheets by the following week, thus enabling the hours on the sheets to be checked against the contract administrator's own records.

Clearly the main thing to watch for if you are a contract administrator is labour being allocated to a variation priced on daywork rates when the contractor is actually working on the contracted work scope. If this happens, and it is not spotted, then the employer might be paying twice for the same work, once by paying the bill rates and once by reimbursing the daywork rates.

Price escalation

Less popular in modern times than it was in times of high inflation, escalation clauses allow contractors to seek reimbursement for the inflationary price increases that affect their costs during the contract period. This is achieved in one of two ways. First, the contractor may allow a fixed price addition to the contract price as a non-adjustable risk item. Second, the employer may adjust tender base date prices to reflect the period in which the work is carried out, usually utilising an agreed formula. There are seldom disagreements in this area unless the contract works overrun significantly or the programmed sequence of the works is severely dislocated. When this happens, the resultant costs of escalation will often be included in a claim for loss and expense.

Loss and expense claims

In Section 1 a number of reasons why claims arise were discussed. These may include the financial consequences of relevant events giving rise to extensions of time under the contract and other loss-bearing contract clauses and breaches of contract by the employer. Later in this section we consider how such losses should be calculated and evaluated.

The JCT terminology 'loss and/or expense' is not defined in the standard form contracts. Any clue as to its meaning is derived from case law. This is discussed in Section 3. Conventionally, loss and expense is deemed to cover those items of expenditure that arise from the progress of the works being materially affected by an act or omission of the employer or the employer's agents. The wording in JCT 2011 at clause 4.23 reads:

> *If in the execution of this Contract the Contractor incurs or is likely to incur direct loss and/or expense for which he would not be reimbursed by a payment under any other provision in these Conditions … the Architect/Contract Administrator shall ascertain, or instruct the Quantity Surveyor to ascertain, the amount of loss and/or expense which has been or is being incurred*

An application for reimbursement of direct loss and/or expense under such circumstances will often contain one or more of the following heads of claim:

- site overheads or preliminaries
- general overheads and head office costs
- profit
- inflation
- loss of productivity or acceleration costs
- finance charges
- costs of preparing the claim.

Valuing prolongation

The problem of valuing site overhead or preliminary costs is usually readily resolved. Preliminary costs will usually include site set-up and mobilisation costs, time-related costs, work- and method-related costs and demobilisation costs.

A three-week extension of time will clearly affect the time-related costs (site staff, accommodation, communications and IT, utilities, security and local levies and taxes) but will rarely affect the mobilisation or demobilisation costs.

The work- or method-related costs may be affected but that depends entirely on the items which have been included in the preliminaries. For example, on some larger projects tower cranes, batching plants and crushing plants may be included in the preliminaries. As noted above, their mobilisation or demobilisation costs will probably not be affected but, unless there has been a significant recovery from variations, there may be some time-related costs to recover under the preliminaries claim.

Once the time-related costs are established, then the calculation should be a simple one. The rule is that the contractor should be fully reimbursed for the expenditure of necessary additional costs. To value this entitlement it may not be appropriate for the preliminary costs in the contract bills simply to be adjusted pro rata. In a period of delay the contractor may need more or fewer staff and more or less accommodation than was properly allowed for in the tender. The secret to a proper evaluation is to understand exactly when, during the project, the delay occurred. It is at this juncture, possibly in the middle of the contract period, where the recoverable loss would arise. In too many simplistic claims the assessment or ascertainment simply seeks to value the costs arising during the prolonged period, that period beyond the completion date. This is clearly not a true measure of the loss.

It is for the architect to decide, on the facts of each case, probably in conjunction with the quantity surveyor, whether the claimed costs are appropriate, citing these principles in their ascertainment.

"It is for the architect to decide whether the claimed costs are appropriate"

Valuing head office contributions, use of formulae

Before embarking on a discussion of head office costs it is worth taking a moment to remember that many of the formulae used to recover such costs, and which gave rise to much legal precedent, were based on construction practices as they were in the 1960s and 1970s.

A modern view

While the views stated in the next three paragraphs are a little radical, and they will not be accepted by everyone, they have been accepted by tribunals around the world when properly explained and linked to basic legal principles.

In the 1960s a site establishment might consist of a site manager, site agent, and foremen with visiting quantity surveyors and bonus/time-and-motion clerks. All administration, procurement, ordering, management and organisation was carried out at the head office. There was no IT to speak of, often there was not even a phone, and critical path planning was still merely a theory. In short, a site usually relied very heavily on the head office staff and facilities.

On modern projects we can have what amounts to a branch office, or regional office, based on the site with IT, draughtsmen, quantity surveyors, planners, payroll, procurement, quality assurance and health and safety personnel, all potentially led at director level. These sites are essentially self-sufficient.

It is my view, and my experience, that if we try to use the tools developed to meet the needs of the 1960s and 1970s to value head office costs half a century later, we will have a claim that massively overvalues the head office loss.

In 2008, as expert witness instructed on a dispute arising from a major infrastructure project in the United Arab Emirates, I was faced with a contractor's claim based on Hudson's formula for the recovery of head office costs. The claim was properly compiled and was mathematically correct in every aspect but one, its outcome. The calculation showed that prolongation had incurred a loss of around $7 million. A quick examination of the contractor's status showed that the project (part of a five-year programme of work) was run entirely from the extensive site office. Essentially, the site establishment was the regional Middle East and Africa office of the Far Eastern contractor. With the exception of two sales personnel employed in offices in the city, the whole regional office was on site and was thus being recovered in the prolongation claim. There was little contact with head office back in the Far East as the region was a profit centre, effectively a subsidiary.

Despite the fact that the formula had been properly calculated and applied it could not, and did not, reflect any loss. It is the true loss or the costs incurred that stand to be valued and only rarely will formulae provide the correct answer.

Having stated my personal views, let us now review the status of the law and the contract on head office loss.

Understanding head office loss

In many contracting organisations the head office exists solely to support the site operations. The accounts department pays the wages of operatives, and head office staff will be engaged in dealing with the effects of prolongation and delay. Of course, it can be argued that the head office and its staff would incur those costs anyway, but this is not how the legal commentators have generally regarded the recovery of such costs. In many contracting organisations, the overheads are budgeted as a percentage of planned turnover and so, if work on one site is prolonged, then personnel are not able to work elsewhere to create that turnover or earn its attached overhead. In short, it is generally accepted that head office overheads are a legitimate head of claim. In the words of the Official Referee in *J.F. Finnegan Ltd v. Sheffield City Council* (1988):

> *it is generally accepted that, on principle, the Contractor who is delayed in completing a contract due to the default of his Employer, may properly have a claim for Head Office or off site overheads during the period of delay on the basis that the workforce, but for the delay, might have had the opportunity of being employed on another contract which would have had the effect of funding the overheads during the overrun period.*

Therefore, to prove that a loss has been incurred the contractor must first prove that, had their resources not been engaged on the overrun of the project in question, they would have deployed those resources elsewhere to fund their overheads. Such a task is not easily accomplished, although the courts have often displayed a certain tolerance towards the contractor's duty.

Two cases are illustrative of the courts' approach. In *Peak Construction (Liverpool) Ltd v. McKinney Foundations Ltd* (1970) Salmon L.J. said: 'possibly some evidence as to what the organisation consisted of, what part of the head office is being referred to, and what they were doing at the material times could be of help'.

In *Tate & Lyle Food and Distribution Ltd v. Greater London Council* (1981) it was held that the plaintiff could, in principle, recover damages for managerial and supervisory expenses directly attributable to the defendant's breaches. On the facts of the particular case the plaintiff's claim failed because of the failure to keep proper records and supporting documentation. In the words of Forbes J.:

> *I have no doubt that the expenditure of managerial time in remedying an actionable wrong done to a trading concern can properly form the subject matter of a head of special damage … I would also accept that it must be extremely difficult to quantify. But modern office arrangements permit the recording of the time spent by managerial staff on particular projects. I do*

*not believe that it would have been impossible for the Plaintiffs in this case to
have kept some record to show the extent to which their trading routine was
disturbed by the necessity for continual dredging sessions … While I am satisfied that this head of damage can properly be claimed, I am not prepared to
advance into an area of pure speculation when it comes to quantum. I feel
bound to hold that the Plaintiffs have failed to prove that any sum is due
under this head.*

In summary, the judges state that contractors should establish exactly who at
head office was provably involved and that there should be a record of their time
spent on the overrunning project.

Formulae

Despite the misgivings of many of those involved in dispute resolution, head
office overheads are often calculated by use of a formula, although, as the judges
have noted above, the contractor's actual loss must be established if recovery is
to be guaranteed.

In my experience as an expert witness, contractors' head office costs are rarely
adequately recorded. To overcome this problem a formula is often deployed to
evaluate the proper allocation of cost. The three main formulae in use are known
as Hudson's, Emden's and Eichleay. The Hudson's and Emden's formulae have both
found very limited judicial and arbitral approval in common law countries whereas
Eichleay has found some favour in the USA. The actual formulae are reproduced
in simple terms below, where HO is head office and OHP is overhead and profit.

Hudson's: (Tender OHP ÷ 100) × (contract sum ÷ period in weeks) × delay in weeks

Emden's: (Actual OHP ÷ 100) × (contract sum ÷ period in weeks) × delay in weeks

Eichleay: (Total project billings ÷ total company billings) × HO OHP = project OHP

Then:

(Contract OHP ÷ no. of days on site) × no. of days of compensable delay

For most commentators, the fundamental weakness of Hudson's formula is
its reliance on the percentage that the contractor has allowed in the tender for
general overheads and which may never have been achieved. Emden's, despite
its limitations, does at least refer to actual figures achieved by the contractor for

annual turnover, profit and overhead costs. The Eichleay formula simply calcu-
lates, pro rata, what proportion of the audited overall company OHP is carried by
the project in the light of its value. That project OHP is then divided to give a daily
rate which is applied to every day of delay.

The use of the Eichleay formula was criticised as inappropriate in *Berley Industries
Inc. v. City of New York* (1978). In that case, 87 per cent of the work had been completed by the due date for completion, leaving only $60,000 worth of work to be
done during a long period of delay. Applying the Eichleay formula would have
resulted in a claim of more than $19,000 for head office overheads. The court
rejected the formula approach on the basis that: 'The mathematical computations
under the [formula] produce a figure with, at best, a chance relationship to actual
damages and, at worst, no relationship at all'; a criticism that could be directed at
any formula method.

Based on the case law, and the wording of the JCT family of contracts, the recommended approach to ascertaining the loss incurred is as follows:

- The contractor should identify and prove the real loss incurred because the
  contract and the courts demand it.
- Should that evidence not be available, then the contractor may as well try a
  formula approach.
- The formula approach may find some acceptance with an adjudicator or
  arbitrator if the results are realistic and proportionate.

The various formulae can be found on the Internet by simply typing their
respective names into a search box. If you prefer to refer to textbooks written by
practitioners, then *The Presentation and Settlement of Contractors' Claims* by Mark
Hackett and Geoffrey Trickey (2001) gives a thorough analysis of each formula and
its strengths and weaknesses.

Oddly, the major construction law books, including *Hudson's* itself, offer very
little support for the formula methods, even to the extent of failing to define the
formula that bears their name.

Loss of profit

Contractors exist to make profits and so most quantity surveyors will consider
including loss of profit on additional work in their ascertainment, if it is properly evidenced. Some contractors, however, will argue that they have lost the

"very persuasive evidence will be required before any judge or arbitrator will consider making an award"

opportunity to earn profit elsewhere as a result of being delayed on an overrunning project. They may assert that they had to turn down a lucrative contract because this project continued to absorb all available staff and labour. If such losses really have been incurred, then very persuasive evidence will be required before any judge or arbitrator will consider making an award. Claims for loss of profit of this type generally arise as part of a common law damages claim for breach of contract and will often be treated as 'special damages' under the second limb of *Hadley v. Baxendale*. The person responsible for ascertainment under JCT 2011 will not be subject to too much criticism if they argue that these 'profits foregone' do not constitute a direct loss and are therefore only ascertainable outside the contractual machinery.

Inflation due to delay

Where a fixed price contract has been awarded and the contract is prolonged beyond the fixed price end date, then the contractor is usually entitled to some recompense. The value of the claim should be the excess necessarily incurred as a direct result of the prolongation. Again, evidence is of paramount importance. Records must be kept to show how labour and material prices were higher when the work was actually carried out compared to the prices prevailing when the work was programmed to be carried out. A common method used by claims advisors (wrongly in my view) is to deduct the fixed price allowance from the tender sum and revert to pricing the whole job on a formula basis. This method usually overcompensates the claimant as well as removing the risk element of price escalation that the contractor agreed to take when the contract was signed. Generally, this methodology should be rejected.

Loss of productivity and acceleration

This head of claim is usually the most difficult to agree, not because of difficulty in pricing, but because of a lack of clearly identifiable evidence. A wise construction QC once told me that there were three simple rules to follow for success before any tribunal. They were keep good records, keep better records and, finally, keep the best records.

Even the basic understanding of the law that can be gained from this guide will show that a contractor is entitled to be reimbursed not only for delays but also for disturbance to the planned progress of the works. JCT 2011 makes this clear in clause 4.23 where it states: 'or because the regular progress of the Works or of any part of them has been or is likely to be materially affected by any of the Relevant Matters'.

So, if the contractor's records clearly demonstrate that they have been financially disadvantaged due to disruption caused by the employer's default then the contractor may seek reimbursement under the contract, even if the project completes on time.

The planned progress of the works is usually accepted as being the agreed contract programme. Ideally, the contractor should demonstrate, using an updated programme, how the disruption affected the programme and the workforce. It is important that the programme used shows the actual progress of the job rather than simply being the tender programme. An updated programme will show those delaying and disruptive events already having an impact on the works at the time the employer causes or is deemed to be responsible for further disruption. This will allow the contractor to assess, honestly, the impact of the employer's disruption while ensuring that they do not claim for problems of their own making.

Many claims for loss of productivity fail because good contemporaneous records do not exist and the contractor can only guess who was to blame for which loss. Those involved in ascertainment must ensure that:

- the disruption and/or delay has been evidenced by reference to current site progress, and
- the cause of the disruption/delay is the liability of the employer, and
- the damage claimed is inextricably linked to the disruption/delay caused.

Another version of the loss of productivity claim is the acceleration claim. Few of the standard forms give the employer's representative the power to instruct a contractor to accelerate the works. So, when assessing a contractor's possible entitlement to extensions of time under the contract, and deciding not make an award, architects should remember that the contractor may impliedly have a duty to accelerate by reason of the wording of the contract; for example, in JCT 2011 clause 2.28.6.1: 'the Contractor shall constantly use his best endeavours to prevent delay in the progress of the Works or any Section, however caused'.

In such cases it has been successfully argued that there was implied instruction to accelerate or to undertake 'constructive acceleration'; that is, to institute such acceleration as is necessary to comply with one's obligations but not otherwise instructed.

One contract that provides expressly for acceleration is the FIDIC form of contract. Clause 46 permits an employer to order a contractor who is in culpable delay to accelerate.

In the absence of a specific contractual provision to cover acceleration, to ensure reimbursement under this head of claim the acceleration methods and associated costs must be agreed between the parties before the work is speeded up. Wary contractors will bear in mind that if the contract has already suffered disruption, then it is highly probable that there will be further disruption during the period of acceleration. This being the case, they will try to make provision in the acceleration agreement for any further delays and disruption before arriving at a cost for acceleration.

Valuing acceleration measures

In some cases the acceleration proceeds without prior agreement on price. If this should happen then the evaluation must be based on the factual evidence available after completion. The procedure for evaluating these losses is broadly the same as for evaluating disruption. Those ascertaining such losses should be aware that there are reasons why the mere process of accelerating the works may cause a drop in productivity. Among these are:

- learning curve for additional operatives
- reduced production due to fatigue and long or unsocial hours
- congestion of working areas
- increased pressure on supervision
- higher proportion of defective work.

"The only reliable way of valuing acceleration is by maintaining excellent contemporaneous records"

The only reliable way of valuing acceleration is by maintaining excellent contemporaneous records of the acceleration efforts. That is, to seek reimbursement for the additional effort expended as a result of implementing acceleration methods and *not* to base reimbursement on achievement.

An acceleration agreement is, by its very nature, an agreement to implement accelerative measures. Usually such measures are undertaken without any express guarantee that completion will be achieved earlier. The courts have examined acceleration agreements on a number of occasions and, even where the outcome expected from the agreement was not fully achieved, it has been held that the client was still obliged to pay, see *Lester Williams v. Roffey Brothers & Nicholls (Contractors) Ltd* (1990).

Valuing disruption

As noted above, the evaluation of disruption is troublesome because the work disrupted is often within the contracted work scope, and variation work is priced at normal bill of quantity rates, yet is carried out in an unproductive fashion. Further difficulty arises when the disrupted work is so intermingled with productive work that it is difficult to separate the two. Let us first dismiss the most obvious and easiest forms of disruptive working:

- standing time
- defined work scope carried out in different conditions.

In some cases the work is disrupted in a way that is easily measured. In 2001, I was asked to value the disruption caused on a London building being reconstructed between two existing buildings. The restaurant on one of the adjoining plots obtained an injunction preventing noisy work and vibration during dining hours. Operatives had to stand down from noon until 2.30 p.m. when they had to be available again to work until 7 p.m. This was easily monitored and valued.

Another instance where the disruption can be managed easily is where a defined work scope is priced to be executed in one set of conditions but has to be executed in different conditions. In 2006, in a shipyard in the Netherlands, I was faced with a situation where the welding of the process pipework should have been carried out in the summer/autumn. It had to be carried out in a bitterly cold winter. We allowed habitats (scaffolding and sheeting) to be erected around the welders with heaters inside. We also adjusted the labour norms to allow for slower progress. With these measures the loss was contained and measured. On any JCT-type building project where the Standard Method of Measurement (SMM) has been used, the quantity surveyor will be able to value work carried out in different conditions or where the character of the work has changed, as long as an instruction is issued. This adjustment can be included in the interim applications, thus avoiding a claim.

Most of the other instances of disrupted working are much more difficult to value and evidence. Nonetheless, the architect or contract administrator can reduce the occurrence and value of any dispute by removing from the dispute any easily determined disruption losses. I would say that if, during the project, the contractor was reimbursed for any additional plant, preliminaries and standing labour that were self-evidently and obviously involved in the disruption, this will be of considerable help later.

In my role as an expert witness I am currently dealing with a £25 million disruption claim on a project that ended over two years ago. Around £15 million of that claim is for items that could have been agreed easily at the time, such as agreed additional plant, additional labour resources, additional preliminary items and so forth. This would have left the trickier lost labour production claims of £10 million to be reported upon by the experts and decided by the tribunal. It should be obvious that expenditure on dealing with these issues at a later date in formal resolution will be significantly greater than it would have been if the disruption had been agreed between the parties.

Valuing lost production, labour, attendant plant and consumables is often very time consuming and does not always produce evidence that is unimpeachable, or even convincing. There are a number of methods for valuing lost production, all of which I have used or considered and all of which would need a separate book to explain fully. The best known are:

- global claim, *quantum meruit* – usually a non-starter
- measured mile – used widely, it compares actual output with tendered output and seeks to establish the difference
- industry norms – this method compares actual output with industry norms and seeks to establish the difference
- past projects – compares outputs with earlier 'similar' projects.

All of these methods have obvious pitfalls, but some have found favour if enough effort has been made to overcome their weaknesses. There are a number of more acceptable methods available to practitioners, which use highly academic statistical and financial analysis models, but these are complex and difficult to summarise. If any reader wants to invest time in reviewing the studies on evaluating disruption, I would suggest the best summaries are available from the AACE (American Association of Cost Engineers) via the Internet.

Occasionally architects will be faced with disruption claims based on the findings of Messrs Horner and Talhounie in the Chartered Institute of Building (CIOB) book *Effects of Accelerated Working, Delays and Disruption on Labour Productivity*. Their findings have merit but they would both admit that limits should be placed on the usefulness of those findings. Essentially, they find that working long hours, unsocial hours, in congested areas, on new projects and with new people will reduce productivity.

There is no simple answer to the question of how to value disruption nor is it likely that you will be expected to value a complex disruption without reference to an expert. The best advice is to assess and value the obvious expenditures and reduce the value to be determined by expensive lawyers and experts.

> *"There is no simple answer to the question of how to value disruption"*

Financing and interest

Commercial debts are covered by the Late Payment of Commercial Debts (Interest) Act 1998. This allows interest to be charged at a set rate, which is the Bank of England base rate plus 8 per cent, from the end of a notional 30-day credit period. For the purposes of this legislation, the Bank of England base rate is fixed every six months. For commercial debts, the legislation allows specified amounts for 'reasonable debt recovery costs'. In practice, of course, few contractors ask for payment of interest (or debt recovery costs) under the legislation unless the dispute is referred to a third party.

If a contractor wishes to pursue a claim for interest they must issue a writ or begin arbitration proceedings. The award of interest is then made at the court rate in High Court and county court proceedings and in arbitration at the discretion of the arbitrator, although the arbitrator would be unwise to depart from the court rate or compound interest without good cause. A judge has the power to award the interest that has accrued from the date the cause of action arose to the date of judgment. This express power is given to judges by a combination of the Law Reform (Miscellaneous Provisions) Act 1934 and the Administration of Justice Act 1982. An implied power to do likewise is also given to arbitrators. Academic lawyers and commentators have pointed out that, as arbitration can be commenced as soon as a payment is late, this remedy should readily permit recovery of full interest on debts.

As well as common law interest and statutory interest awarded as part of the damages in litigation and arbitration, courts and arbitrators accept that contractors may incur additional damages as a result of an interruption of their cash flow. A major part of the loss and expense suffered by any claimant may arise from a loss of potential interest or as an expenditure on overdraft interest. In many cases these 'financing charges' are allowed by judges and arbitrators and are awarded as a part of the contractor's loss and expense claim.

In *F. G. Minter Ltd v. Welsh Health Technical Services Organisation* (1980) it was held that interest is recoverable by a contractor under the JCT forms if it represents those financing charges included in the contractor's loss and expense claim. This is still the case over 30 years later.

The Minter decision was followed by the Court of Appeal in the later case of *Rees & Kirby*, where the court held that:

- financing charges can be compounded
- financing charges do not accrue during an intervening event, such as when a contractor suspends their application during settlement talks
- financing charges do not apply to breaches by the architect where they fail to certify within the stipulated time.

A contractor will often include in their claim an application for interest on liquidated and ascertained damages previously, albeit wrongfully, levied. While claims consultants may disagree, it is arguable that an employer who deducts liquidated and ascertained damages, provided they do not fall foul of the notice provisions and conditions precedent to deduction, is not in breach of contract if the architect subsequently grants an extension of time. Clause 2.32.3 of JCT 2011 says:

> *If the Architect/Contract Administrator fixes a later Completion Date for the Works or a Section or such later Completion Date is stated in a Confirmed Acceptance, the Employer shall pay or repay to the Contractor any amounts recovered, allowed or paid under clause 2.32 for the period up to that later Completion Date.*

Any employer or architect considering a contractor's claim for interest following the repayment of liquidated and ascertained damages under JCT 2011 should point to this strict wording as a defence. What appears to be agreed by the parties is a contractual repayment without any right to interest.

Claim preparation costs

As a general rule the contractor's staff will prepare the claim as the work proceeds and the preparation costs will be recovered in the preliminaries or overheads. Where the work is done in a period of prolongation, the costs are recovered under the same heads in the prolongation claim. However, there are cases where, despite the best efforts of the contractor to evidence loss and expense, the client's representatives fail to carry out their obligation under the contract to ascertain the losses. In these circumstances, if the contractor is put to a cost which is unreasonable and is not otherwise recoverable they may wish to seek reimbursement on the grounds of the failure of the client's representatives.

Architects should protect the employer by ensuring that the employer's quantity surveyor is acting reasonably in the ascertainment and is not placing a burden of proof on the contractor which is not demanded by the contract or the law. Some inexperienced, or perhaps cynical, quantity surveyors seem to believe or suggest that contractors must prove their case 'beyond reasonable doubt'. This erroneous view may result in the employer bearing unnecessary legal costs when the courts find for the contractor who has properly demonstrated entitlement on the 'balance of probabilities'.

A further problem arises when outside claim specialists are employed to prepare a claim. In these cases the principles remain the same; their costs will only be recoverable if the employer's representatives have failed in their duty properly to ascertain the loss and expense and the outside consultant has been employed to do the work instead. Generally, however, the costs of claims specialists are not recoverable unless they are acting in relation to case preparation and presentation in arbitration or are instructed to act as expert witnesses in either litigation or arbitration.

SUMMARY

Loss and expense claims are difficult to evaluate. There is never any substitute for good record-keeping and an understanding of the legal and contractual principles underlying such claims. Realism and honesty should make claims more readily acceptable and so enable the client to settle them more quickly. In addition, any claim must be presented to the certifier in a manner which is readable and concise.

Here are a few tips for certifiers that have been collated from the experiences of quantity surveyors, claims consultants, expert witnesses and others involved in the defence of claims:

- Always seek evidence before accepting claims; do not rely on estimates or allowances to establish costs incurred when records should be available.
- Ensure that any evidence offered in support of a loss is objective and from a reliable source; preferably, contemporaneous documents should be produced.
- If contemporaneous documents are not available, then industry accepted publications may offer a safe alternative. Do not rely on unfamiliar documentation such as price lists or catalogues as these can be misleading.
- Do not accept formula methods of evaluation without expert advice.
- Ask questions until you have been answered fully and satisfactorily.
- Seek guidance from others if the evaluation of a claimed loss falls outside of your area of expertise.
- Remember always that once you have asked for information and it has been properly provided you will show prejudice if you ignore it or dismiss it. If it would satisfy a tribunal it should satisfy you.
- Answer all claims and correspondence politely and courteously and ensure that anyone reviewing your words later will see that you have an open mind.

Certifiers must maintain the moral high ground and show the world that they have acted reasonably. If they do this they will be treated kindly by any tribunal.

Section 6
False claims do happen

In this Section:

- *Dishonesty and theft*
- *The Fraud Act 2006*
- *Loss and expense claims*

Dishonesty and theft

We have now covered how a loss and expense claim should be valued but, before we move on to how such claims should be presented, assessed and agreed, it is important to understand how vital honesty in claiming is to our integrity, and our freedom.

In 1986 I was the commercial manager for a company acting as a major sub-contractor on a significant building project in Greater London. The project was overrunning and, despite our best efforts, we were being delayed by others but we were not being awarded any extensions of time. At the end of the month we received a 'set off' notice from the contractor which stated, 'because you are in delay you must bear a proportion of the prolongation costs including site establishment, security, rates, water, lighting' etc., etc. There then followed a calculation of the 'set off' which essentially showed that 20 per cent of the overrun costs were due to our failures.

Notwithstanding the fact that we were not liable and so owed nothing, since the delays were imposed by others, the sum allegedly owed – several thousand pounds – was duly deducted from our certified payments. There were 39 subcontractors on site and I contacted every one and compiled a dossier. The contractor was deducting between 5 and 20 per cent of the site establishment costs from us all, so a total in excess of 400 per cent of their asserted site costs were being 'set off'. As the only subcontractor's representative with a law degree, I was asked by the others to pursue the contractor. I did, with righteous indignation! Despite the pleas of the quantity surveyor, his manager, the project manager and the regional director, I refused to discuss the matter with them. Their increasingly desperate defences of 'It was an honest mistake', 'OK then, it was a try on', 'Look, no harm was done' fell on deaf ears. I drafted a report for the police evidencing their systematic fraud and sent it to the group MD of the contracting organisation asking for his comment before we, the subcontractors, submitted it to the police.

The MD apologised personally to all subcontractors and sacked everyone responsible. All monies were returned and no payment or retention was ever late again.

In 2006, while preparing an expert witness report on a retail park dispute for the architect, the quantity surveyor and their employer, I was obliged to do the same again when I discovered that the contractor had forged invoices to supplement his claim. The prepared police report obliged the contractor to withdraw all claims, valid or not. The contractor was struck off the partnering list of a major developer, and all for the sake of stealing a few thousand pounds.

"quantity surveyors from across the UK have served time in prison for making false claims"

Until recently these offences were covered by the Theft Acts and quantity surveyors from across the UK have served time in prison for making false claims. It is a dangerous thing to do and yet, as I have noted, it still happens.

Contractors, or other claimants, must be honest in their pursuit of purported loss, while architects and certifiers must be honest in their assessments and certifications. Not to be so is even more dangerous in today's aggressive and litigious environment.

The Fraud Act 2006

In the 1980s these types of fraud, perpetrated in construction claims, were covered by the Theft Act 1968, where 'obtaining pecuniary advantage by deception' was included at section 16. As a result of some archaic wording, it was not always obvious to the layman where the boundaries lay between exaggeration and theft. However, since the Fraud Act 2006 came into force, the offences we sometimes see embodied in construction claims are more clearly defined. Consider the generality and clarity of these words:

A person is guilty of fraud if he … dishonestly makes a false representation, and intends, by making the representation – to make a gain for himself or another, or to cause loss to another or to expose another to a risk of a loss.

Does that wording taken directly from the Act sound like it might describe a claim you have seen in the past? Or, indeed, does it sound like one on your desk right now? It certainly describes many of the claims I see. The wording is clarified further in the Act, leaving even less room for argument: 'A representation is false if – it is untrue or misleading, and the person making it knows that it is, *or might be*, untrue or misleading' [emphasis added].

To understand that a claimant may be guilty of perpetrating a fraud in submitting a claim for money, or time (in order to avoid liquidated and ascertained damages), without proper evidence is deeply worrying. But to know that a claimant may also be liable if a statement they made proves to be untrue and they knew that it *might be* misleading or untrue should be alarming to some claimants.

Loss and expense claims

In so many instances, I see formally submitted quantum claims that are advanced on precisely the basis described above. In such cases the claimant making the representation does not have the evidence to show a loss and so relies on a 'demonstration' of loss, knowing that it is not true or at the very least *might be untrue*. These claimants are not generally dishonest, they simply rely on the fact that the respondent has a right of reply and so in the end a negotiated settlement will probably be reached that more closely reflects the real loss incurred.

Within the past year a client who had suffered a loss of some £4 million on a project asked his claims consultant, in my presence, to 'get the claim up to £5 million to give me some scope to come down'. I convinced the client such action was unnecessary. Over the past 18 years spent in the disputes arena I have consistently argued that claims should be valid, accurate, honest and rigorously negotiated. In my experience, building 'loss leaders' or 'negotiating margin' into claims almost inevitably leads to a loss of confidence in the valuation of the true losses.

Given the wording of the Fraud Act 2006 reproduced above, the exaggeration of claims alone may lead to prosecution and imprisonment. So, altering documents to suggest that a loss has been incurred, or manipulating programmes to demonstrate an extension of time that is not due, thus depriving the employer of liquidated damages, is quite simply madness.

SUMMARY

Honesty and thoroughness are the best defence to claims of fraud. If we ensure that all claims are properly researched and professionally assembled, with reliable evidence, we can be sure that we have acted within the law.

Section 7
How loss and expense claims should be presented

In this Section:

- *The written claim*
- *Presentation*
- *Be concise and clear*
- *Evidence and legal argument*
- *Tactics*

The written claim

Since the mid-1990s there has been an emphasis on attempts to keep costs down in arbitration and litigation. The judiciary have made it clear that they wish to see the parties making more use of documentary evidence in place of lengthy oral presentations. In most cases, barristers are now expected to submit either a skeleton argument or a full opening statement in writing for the judge or arbitrator to read before the hearing. Written witness statements and expert witness reports are also exchanged by the parties and provided to the judge or arbitrator in advance of the hearing, with the documents referred to in the body of the statement appended. This practice, long adopted in arbitration, is now well-established in the courts. The purpose of these procedural changes and others in regard to expert witnesses is that time-consuming evidence in chief can be reduced to a minimum and the traditional recourse to 'trial by ambush' avoided. Although arbitration conducted by documents alone will only ever be possible in

"A simpler and better prepared claim does help to keep court costs down by reducing the length of hearings"

the least complex cases, the number of matters dealt with in this way is growing. A simpler and better prepared claim does help to keep court costs down by reducing the length of hearings. Associated costs, such as those relating to legal representation and experts, would similarly be reduced.

Sharing a taxi with a Law Lord after a conference on arbitration law, the eminent retired judge asked me if I had a question I wanted to ask as I had him as a captive audience for the next few minutes. I asked about how we could simplify claims and pleadings. He replied that he had never encountered a construction case that could not be summarised on four sides of A4 paper. Experience had presumably taught him that some of the people involved in the litigation process were unduly long-winded. There are three techniques that can assist a claimant in the presentation of their claims which will not only satisfy the needs of the certifier but which should also find favour with those considering the merits of a claim in the case of a dispute, whether they be judge or arbitrator. They are:

- high quality of presentation
- conciseness and clarity
- properly evidenced arguments and contentions.

These virtues should encourage you, as a certifier, an architect or quantity surveyor, to be more accepting of the contractor's claim. However, although presentational techniques are important and form part of the art of persuasion, it is essential for certifiers not to be blinded to the imperfections and incoherence of a claim by the impression it creates when taken at face value.

Presentation

With the common use of desktop publishing and the variety of fonts available in word processing, it is now possible for contractors to produce high-quality documents which are of publication standard. Claimants should assist the certifier by integrating into the text various graphics, such as spreadsheets, tables, charts and photographs. Construction professionals can now produce, at their own desks, very complex compilations of information and artwork which formerly would have taken many weeks to prepare. As a result, even the smaller contractor has the ability to produce a document that not only reads well but which also includes supporting histograms, graphs, diagrams and sketches. 'A picture paints a thousand words' may be a cliché, but in the context of good claims preparation illustrative material can convey to the certifier, a judge or arbitrator a complex point more clearly than a long prose narrative. For example, three-dimensional computer graphics are now commonly used to re-create projects to highlight the impact of delay and disruption on the anticipated programme.

It is my view that every claim you receive should have a title page and a contents page and be bound in such a way that the pages lie flat on the desk for easy reference. The claim should be broken down into sections which clearly state the substance of the case. The headings should be presented with their appropriate page number in the contents section; they can be hyperlinked in electronic versions. In the event that a claim does ultimately go to arbitration or litigation, barristers and judges prefer to have each paragraph numbered with a unique reference to allow rapid identification at the hearing.

Colour should be used to help make the document look more appealing. For easy reference, charts, graphs and tables are best sited in the text at the points where they are most relevant, rather than as appendix material. Clearly, this is not always possible and so the use of a companion volume containing the appendices will prevent the claim document being too bulky and uninviting. The certifier is free to communicate to the claimant that a well-drafted, tribunal-friendly document will always have an advantage over a poorly drafted claim that is less accessible.

It is a fact that, while many barristers and judges deal with construction cases regularly, they are not always able to visualise the problems that have occurred on a site, and even a technical arbitrator may be unsure if new techniques, materials or methods have been used in the construction. To assist non-construction professionals to understand the problems that have arisen, any claim or defence document should include pictures in the form of good quality

"any claim or defence document should include pictures"

colour photographs and video. Contractors should be made aware that a helpful, high-quality presentation will not only be a great help to the architect or certifier but it may also earn the employer's gratitude and future custom.

Certifiers can reasonably expect any claim to be brief while setting out the case fully and clearly in the minimum number of words. The temptation for contractors is to subject the architect, claims assessor, judge or arbitrator to a deluge of photocopied documents; this should be discouraged. Hopefully, claimants are becoming aware that certifiers, judges and arbitrators have the same limitations on their attention span as everyone else, and when confronted with a claim that runs to three full lever-arch files they will be tempted to skim through the text to find the parts they consider important and, as a result, they may miss some essential point. All parties need to understand that by keeping the presentation documents to a few pages, properly numbered and punctuated and supported by charts and diagrams, a contractor or claims advisor is actively encouraging the certifier to consider the document in its entirety, instead of homing in on those parts which appear most interesting or accessible. Conversely, by presenting a document that is neither concise nor clear, the claimant risks not only alienating the architect but also doing a disservice to an otherwise well-evidenced claim.

In all communication it is important for the claimant and respondent to use plain English and avoid, as far as possible, jargon and specialist terminology. Technical words should be explained in full; a glossary can be included if necessary. The contractor's aim should be to convey the strengths of their case to the architect or assessor, and through them to the client, as clearly as possible. An excellent test of the effectiveness of any claim or response is to invite a complete outsider to review it, comment on its presentation and content, and act as 'devil's advocate'. The different emphases that individuals will place on the same written document can be surprising. The writer's intention must be to ensure that everyone who reads the document will draw only one conclusion: the same conclusion that the architect or quantity surveyor will draw.

Be concise and clear

Most contractors appreciate that, while good presentation and clear and precise text will ensure the best possible start to the process of claims resolution, ultimately these aspects are less important than the content of the claim itself, which must support the case and convince the architect or assessor of its merits. It is up to the claimant to provide clear evidence in a form which is ultimately acceptable to any certifier or adjudicating tribunal and the certifier should be quick to point this out.

"It is up to the claimant to provide clear evidence in a form which is ultimately acceptable to any certifier"

Every claim, and its subsequent response, must contain:

- the particulars of the parties involved in the dispute
- the roles of the parties in the dispute
- the name and details of the originator of the document
- an explanation of the dispute, including any relevant contractual details
- a statement of events, particularly those which gave rise to the dispute.

The claim should additionally state the following:

- the effect of any breaches on the claimant's work or performance
- how the claimant's performance was hindered by the breach
- how the costs incurred relate to the breach
- a full quantification of the damage incurred
- a conclusion stating the sums of monies claimed.

The response should:

- acknowledge or dispute any stated facts
- accept or dispute any evaluation
- explain the certifier's own evaluation, if any, and
- conclude by stating the sum of monies (or amount of additional time) believed to be due, if any.

Case law, including *Wharf Properties Ltd and Another v. Eric Cumine Associates (No. 2)* (1991) and *ICI plc v. Bovis Construction Ltd and Others* (1992), indicates that if the case is not pleaded with full particularity, showing cause and effect, the courts may consider it an abuse of the process and strike the case out either in its entirety or in part. At best, time will be wasted as the architect, assessor or tribunal sends the claim back for clarification or further analysis.

The claimant is usually personally responsible for drafting, or employing a claims consultant to draft, the original claim document. This may later be relied upon by counsel to plead the case if formal proceedings in litigation or arbitration become necessary following a failure to negotiate an acceptable settlement. It is quite likely that any inaccuracies or untruths included in the original claim document, particularly exaggerated figures put forward as the contractor's losses, will appear in the pleadings too. For this reason contractors and all claims consultants should be reminded that a claim document drafted for the purpose of negotiation only is unlikely to be suitable for litigation or arbitration. Prior to submitting any claim document to counsel for pleading, the claimant would be well-advised to review the document to ensure that every statement, fact and figure can be substantiated by witnesses of fact or by reference to documents. Particular attention should be paid to the quantification of alleged losses. If the architect and quantity surveyor have already rejected the claim for lack of evidence or lack of cause and effect, this should act as a warning in terms of the persuasiveness of the claim.

"Ultimately, an unresolved claim will rely on people"

Mention of witnesses of fact leads me to the matter of witness statements and their preparation. Ultimately, an unresolved claim will rely on people; quantity surveyors, site agents, estimators and so forth, who will prove its legitimacy by personal recollection before a judge or arbitrator. Much of the guidance concerning claims preparation also applies to witness statements. These should be clear, concise and in the language of the person who is giving the statement. Witnesses may have to undergo cross-examination on their statements at some future trial or arbitration hearing. It is very important that statements reflect witnesses' true opinions, otherwise, unless they are expert liars, they will be discredited by persistent cross-examination from the other party's counsel. It is in everyone's interests to ensure that there is the same level of accuracy in the witness statements as in the claim document. To pursue or defend a case on the basis of falsehood will cause costs to escalate unnecessarily for everyone. If the claimant's case fails, they may bear the burden not only of the lost claim but also of both their own costs and the costs of the other party. This prospect is not restricted to irresponsible claimants; irresponsible respondents will find themselves in a similar position. Too many claims are prosecuted or defended because individuals ignore the underlying reality of the facts until very late in the process. By then it is too late to avoid high costs of lawyers and expert witnesses.

Evidence and legal argument

As well as being clear, concise and well-prepared, the claim document should be honest and cogent so that the architect or quantity surveyor who receives it will be prompted to discuss terms of settlement. That said, undue credence should not be given by architects or assessors to a well-presented but poorly evidenced claim. When a four-volume claim arrives liberally laced with charts, formulae, graphs and a mass of calculations, it is easy to assume that because so many documents are being presented, there must be some substance to the argued case.

The question that certifiers need to ask is: how much hard evidence is there to support the arguments of the claimant?

I have listed above what should be included in a claim, but to what extent should the claimant set out to prove or substantiate their allegations? In theory, no claim should survive if evidence is unavailable, but in practice many do and are paid because they give the appearance of solidity and legal entitlement. Architects and claims assessors need to ensure that they are only allowing those claims that are, on the balance of probabilities, proved, seeking advice from outside experts if necessary.

Evidence can be actual, suggested or simply absent from an apparently well-presented claim. Actual evidence is provided by the inclusion of contemporary documentation and will include letters, drawings, specifications and instructions. It will also arise from the records of conversations and from data relating to formal and informal meetings.

Suggestive evidence can be presented in the form of charts, histograms and graphs which demonstrate the probable sequence of events. If the charts are based on actual evidence then they in turn become actual evidence. If they are extrapolations from actual data then they become suggested evidence. Should a chart present information not available to all parties at the time (an example might be tendered hours) then it should be treated cautiously, as it may not be real evidence at all. Formulae are one of the best known methods of presenting suggested evidence. By using historical data or researched criteria it is possible to demonstrate that the outcome could have been A (but it is important not to lose sight of the fact that the outcome could equally well have been B). The better the underlying records, the greater the value of the interpolated, extrapolated or calculated result. It is not unknown for claimants to create the illusion of evidence where in reality no evidence exists. There are two common methods of achieving this:

- *constant repetition*: if something is said enough times it must be true
- *bulk*: a thick volume suggests great depth and research.

Assessors should always look beneath the surface and examine the foundations on which the claim is built. Statements should not be accepted as facts; they should be questioned and examined in detail. Architects may find that the claim is absolutely correct and further monies are due to the contractor, but the time has still been well spent if monies can be certified with a clear conscience, with full confidence that a professional job has been done.

Tactics

Certifiers should watch out for the following tactics:

- The use of persuasive language without attendant facts, for example: as *you know* the deliveries were held up because of the late drawing issue and, *as has been well reported*, steel prices rose by 16 per cent in that period.
- The extrapolation of, and use of, published research data well beyond the bounds recommended by the researchers, or beyond a point that makes reasonable sense.
- Concentration on one particular aspect of the claim, perhaps the reasons for a particular delay, while other equally important aspects are glossed over. This usually suggests weakness or a lack of evidence in those other areas.
- Reliance on information that is not in the public domain. This may include a contractor's job costing information, internally issued programmes and so forth.

Theories being paraded as facts or evidence abound in the claims arena. It is essential to evaluate properly the substantiating documentation to ensure that it provides reasonable evidence for the case put forward.

SUMMARY

In short, contractors will sometimes provide beautifully presented, bulky and convincingly worded claims. It is for the assessor or architect to:

- check the facts
- assess the evidence
- ensure causal links are valid, and
- ignore the cosmetic presentation and focus on the bare claim beneath.

It must be clear to most certifiers by now that it is unlikely that even the most unmeritorious claim will be successfully rebutted by a simple refusal to pay. Some negotiation will be necessary. The way in which both parties approach the negotiation will, in large part, determine how much of the claim is paid and that will be discussed in Section 8.

Section 8
The negotiation of loss and expense claims

In this Section:

- *Negotiation defined*
- *Preparing to negotiate a loss and expense claim*
- *People*
- *Behaviour*
- *Tactics*
- *Agreements in writing*

Negotiation defined

One definition of negotiation is that it is a process by which opposing views can be overcome, avoided or compromised. My preferred definition is that negotiation is the coming together of two or more parties, who hold conflicting views, for the purpose of reaching agreement.

The real aim of any negotiation should be to achieve a harmonious settlement and not to alienate the opponent, settle grievances or pursue personal egotistical objectives. There is so much more to negotiation than diplomacy, simple bargaining or compromise, and yet many claims for loss and expense are undertaken using one of these naive approaches. Architects and assessors should be aware that compromise tends to favour the stronger or more determined party and so it should be avoided.

"There is so much more to negotiation than diplomacy, simple bargaining or compromise"

Why negotiate at all, it might be asked? After all, the contracts do not contemplate a negotiated outcome. The simple answer is that while the contracts define in general terms the rights and obligations of the parties and provide the mechanism for obtaining legal remedies – they impose no obligation to negotiate – only a rich and/or foolish person will ignore negotiation and launch straight into adjudication, arbitration or litigation.

There are a number of reasons why parties should consider negotiating:

- someone may have done something wrong, possibly even unlawful, and wrong-doers pay heavily in court and in arbitration
- it is always wise to maintain good relationships for the future
- the necessary funding of resources to support litigation or arbitration may be lacking
- there will be a delay in the case coming to trial or final hearing.

"A properly constructed and managed negotiation can give better results in a fraction of the time it takes to litigate or arbitrate"

A properly constructed and managed negotiation can give better results in a fraction of the time it takes to litigate or arbitrate. It can also be done for a fraction of the cost.

If negotiation is such a viable approach, how should it be properly conducted? A fourfold plan of action is the answer:

- prepare
- understand
- negotiate
- agree.

The first two actions should be undertaken before meeting the other side, and the remaining two should be handled amicably in discussions.

Preparing to negotiate a loss and expense claim

Preparing to negotiate a loss and expense claim requires a great deal of research. It will be necessary to identify the real issues behind the claim, as these are not always stated. The other preparations that can be made in advance of a meeting include:

- checking the claim arithmetically; it is surprising how many claims are mathematically flawed, sometimes to a significant degree

- checking the evidence provided; is it real, contemporaneous and reliable? Many claimants rely on spreadsheets that are unsupported by evidence
- examining every area of weakness or absence of proof; these should be assessed, evaluated and listed
- taking time to consider how the claimant will respond to comments from the claims assessor and trying to have a reply ready
- making every effort to understand the contractor's allegations and carefully preparing any rebuttal argument necessary.

 In any negotiation, knowledge is power.

Understanding the case that is presented by the contractor and how to respond effectively is absolutely essential. The claims assessor should:

> *"Understanding the case is absolutely essential"*

- examine all of the documents and charts
- seek to understand the logic and the correlation between the documents and the arguments
- contact the contractor and ask for an explanation if a query arises on a chart or a formula – any failure to understand the documents or follow the contractor's reasoning does not place the claims assessor at fault; it is more likely that the fault lies with the claimant.

All parties should be clear about what they want from the negotiation. It is advisable for all parties to have a 'dry run' to iron out any disagreements within the negotiating team because it is essential to present a united, confident and well-prepared front to the other party in the negotiation.

Having researched and understood the claim, and having prepared properly, the architect or quantity surveyor should be ready to negotiate. The purpose of the negotiation is to find the right solution to the problem, not to remain tied to a predetermined ideal. Parties should be ready to listen, concede valid points and make financial allowances if appropriate. It is to be hoped that somewhere in between the parties' expectations will be a margin for agreement. Whether it is closer to one side's expectations or the other's is irrelevant, as long as the right price is paid for the work

> *"Somewhere in between the parties' expectations will be a margin for agreement"*

done. The parties to a negotiation should be given an opportunity to explain their case in a clear and reasoned way, before giving the other side an opportunity to point out any errors or misconceptions.

Tactical negotiation is prevalent in the construction industry, with parties some-times resorting to coercion, blackmail and threats. If such tactics are used, the party subjected to them should make it clear that they cannot be influenced by disreputable behaviour of this kind and can only be persuaded by cogent argument.

Not all negotiations have a negotiating margin and one side may have to give way. When this is the case it should be achieved by concession and counter-concession so that one side does not feel damaged or abused. Poor deals seldom stick and can often turn into vitriolic litigation. If agreement is to be reached then it should be by proposal and counter-proposal, brainstorming or, only as a last resort, compromise.

The proposal/counter-proposal method is commonplace in loss and expense negotiations. A contractor will submit a claim and provide the reasoning behind it. The client side will point out errors in the reasoning, the arithmetic or the perceived legal basis to the claim. The contractor will consider these points, allow for them and resubmit the case. After a series of such interchanges the gaps are narrowed to a point where agreement is possible. This is probably the most appropriate method for negotiating claims.

Occasionally, there seems to be no scope for reaching agreement because the parties are too far apart. This is often because they have taken up entrenched positions. A golden rule for success is to negotiate outcomes, not positions. There are two reasons. First, neither party has to climb down from a stated position; second, most commercial parties should really be interested in the outcome and not in defeating the other side. After all, these are mere skirmishes, not battles.

> *"A golden rule for success is to negotiate outcomes, not positions"*

It may seem strange that compromise is not recommended as a method of reaching agreement, but this is a matter of understanding the underlying psychology. With compromise neither side can really know what was achievable, and once the euphoria of settlement has ebbed away, a grumbling dissatisfaction often remains. Did they get the best deal possible? Did they leave money on the table?

Were they deceived? These niggling doubts are less likely to persist when agreement has been reached by a more thorough and investigative approach.

Once agreement is reached, the parties should record it in writing as soon as possible. This prevents backsliding and helps those with selective memories to remember both the good and bad points of the agreement. A written agreement of this nature will also be good evidence should a dispute arise later.

There will always be a time when good preparation is simply not enough to avoid a heated dispute, and in these cases it may be advisable to bring in a neutral third party to mediate the dispute or carry out one of the other alternative dispute resolution (ADR) processes. The role that a neutral third party can fulfil is discussed in Sections 9 and 10, along with the traditional methods of dispute resolution: arbitration and litigation.

Before we move on from negotiation let us consider the three main hidden elements of any negotiation and how we can manage them. These elements are people, behaviour and tactics.

People

Every negotiation involves people – not companies, practices or professional bodies but people, individuals. These individuals will all have different character traits, different personal goals and each will have a different level of inter-personal skill.

"Every negotiation involves people, individuals"

People will generally have attributes selected from one or more of the basic personality groups. Some will be aggressive, some assertive, some will be passive and some submissive.

In my book *Conflicts in Construction*, I use the following diagram to explain my view:

	People oriented	Task oriented	
Assertive	Entertainer	**Ruler**	**Aggressive**
Passive	*Admirer*	Analytic	**Submissive**

An individual of the left-hand side will be keen to make friends and keep people happy. An individual on the right-hand side will tend to be less worried about relationships and more concerned about facts. Individuals above the line will want to present or be in control, individuals below the line will tend to be happy to listen or provide data.

If you want to build rapport, as you should in a negotiation, you need to identify what type of character you are negotiating with and act accordingly. In simple terms:

- A ruler wants to be acknowledged as being powerful and important, so acknowledging their status will help you to minimise their aggression and build rapport. You can be as direct as you wish with a ruler.
- An analytic, on the other hand, may crumble under pressure and so gentle enquiries into their data, with the occasional compliment about their research, will endear them to you and get you the answers you need.
- An entertainer will want to be your friend and their greatest fear is that they are disliked or that their data is wrong. Treat the entertainer well, listen to their jokes and ask them to explain their case, but sit back – it may take some time!
- An admirer is the passive version of the entertainer; they will rarely be a main player in a negotiation, but to make them an ally, thank them for their contribution, no matter how small. You could have a friend for life.

It is also helpful to identify where on the chart you appear; this may affect, or at least explain, how you react to the opposition in meetings.

Behaviour

Experienced negotiators can be accomplished actors and, like all good actors, can fake emotions they do not feel. Assume that histrionics, despair, elation, loss, sadness and joy are all part of the act and concentrate on the facts rather than the behaviour of the opposition.

Just as you should not be diverted by behaviour, real or synthetic, you should not be affected by tactics either.

Tactics

There are a number of tactics used in negotiation that are as unacceptable as they are insincere, but they often work and so are repeated. I will highlight a few here because the reason why they work is that people do not always recognise them as tactics.

"There are a number of tactics used in negotiation that are as unacceptable as they are insincere"

- *The wince*: when you make a sensible offer or proposal your opposite number may wince, accompanied by a sharp intake of breath. You may think you have gone too far, have insulted him, your proposal is going to cause him great discomfort. It is a tactic, ignore it. Repeat the proposal and ask for a response.
- *Silence*: again this behaviour is meant to make you feel uncomfortable in the hope that you will fill the silence with a concession. Don't offer a concession; fill the silence by repeating your proposal and await an answer.
- *Lack of authority*: they want to take your offer to a higher authority (who will reject it) in the hope you will make a better offer. Don't improve your offer, simply ask the higher authority to attend the meeting.
- *Trial ballooning*: 'Could you see your way clear to allowing a six-week extension of time?' You agree and they say, 'Well that isn't enough for us but as you are at six weeks and we are at ten … '. This is a sneaky tactic to get you to expose your best bargaining position and then to use it as your new base position.

There are many others, including the heavy-duty tactics of coercion and black-mail. Do not succumb, be bold and have the matter decided on the facts alone.

Agreements in writing

Once an agreement has been reached on any part of the discussion, reduce it to writing and read back your words for agreement. This prevents backtracking later. It also prevents a scurrilous negotiator agreeing nothing until the end and dis-couraging you by stating that no progress has been made and that you need to start again next time. Another tactic, this one is known as 'time pressurisation'.

All agreements should be written clearly, signed and copied before you part. This pre-vents fake misunderstandings and having your opponent nibble away at the agreement.

"All agreements should be written clearly, signed and copied before you part"

SUMMARY

The ideal negotiation is between honest individuals who set a standard for their behaviour, who build a rapport and who eschew tactics. I suggest smiling and showing interest in the opposition, looking for shared interests. Negotiate assertively and acknowledge errors, and accept apologies gracefully.

If you do this and prepare properly, understand the facts and figures, behave well and show magnanimity in victory, you will have the best chance of avoiding formal dispute resolution.

Of course, you will not be able to settle every dispute by means of negotiation, as there will be instances where the claimant will have unrealistic expectations, be intransigent, or both. In these cases third party involvement in any resolution may become necessary. In the next section I address the most common of these methods, adjudication.

Section 9
Adjudication

In this Section:

- *Legislation*
- *The adjudication provisions*
- *Adjudication in practice*

Legislation

Governed by the Housing Grants, Construction and Regeneration Act (HGCRA) 1996, Part II, Construction Contracts, and the Local Democracy, Economic Development and Construction Act (LDEDCA) 2009, section 8, Construction Contracts, adjudication is a formal method of dispute resolution which is binding but not final. An award made in adjudication is subject to a final determination in arbitration or litigation and so can be reviewed and overturned, unless the parties agree otherwise.

"An award made in adjudication can be reviewed and overturned"

The attractions of adjudication are that it does not need lawyers or experts (though many still use both), it is time constrained, it relies on documents only (often but not always), it utilises experts in the field as adjudicators and it can be inexpensive.

Very briefly, the HGCRA 1996, as amended and added to by the LDEDCA 2009, sets out provisions for the proper payment of contractors involved in construction contracts. The provisions of the legislation apply to everyone covered by the Act and will supersede their own contractual arrangements if they conflict with the Act's. In short, as with all legislation, you cannot contract out of the Act if it would otherwise apply to your construction operations.

This means that where the Act conflicts with the terms of any JCT or NEC contract, the Act will prevail. In response to the LDEDCA 2009, which came into force on 1 October 2011, the JCT have rewritten their contracts to comply with the Act, hence the JCT 2011 stable of forms. Similarly, the NEC has also amended its forms. Those using the NEC will know that section W2 of NEC 3 was devised to incorporate the provisions of the 1996 Act.

While it is not within the scope of this book to explain the Construction Acts in detail, it may be useful to explain how the Acts will affect the JCT forms and architects and certifiers generally. I will begin by explaining how adjudication works.

The adjudication provisions

JCT Standard Building Contract with Quantities 2011 allows, at clause 9.2, for adjudication under the Scheme for Construction Contracts. The Scheme also provides a fallback position under the Construction Acts for those contracts that do not contain specific provisions covering (1) to (4) below:

HGCRA 1996, s. 108 (as amended) Right to refer disputes to adjudication

(1) *A party to a construction contract has the right to refer a dispute arising under the contract for adjudication under a procedure complying with this section.*

For this purpose "dispute" includes any difference.

(2) *The contract shall —*

(a) *enable a party to give notice at any time of his intention to refer a dispute to adjudication;*

(b) *provide a timetable with the object of securing the appointment of the adjudicator and referral of the dispute to him within 7 days of such notice;*

(c) *require the adjudicator to reach a decision within 28 days of referral or such longer period as is agreed by the parties after the dispute has been referred;*

(d) *allow the adjudicator to extend the period of 28 days by up to 14 days, with the consent of the party by whom the dispute was referred;*

(e) *impose a duty on the adjudicator to act impartially; and*

(f)   enable the adjudicator to take the initiative in ascertaining the facts and the law.

(3)   The contract shall provide in writing that the decision of the adjudicator is binding until the dispute is finally determined by legal proceedings, by arbitration (if the contract provides for arbitration or the parties otherwise agree to arbitration) or by agreement.

The parties may agree to accept the decision of the adjudicator as finally determining the dispute.

(4)   The contract shall also provide that the adjudicator is not liable for anything done or omitted in the discharge or purported discharge of his functions as adjudicator unless the act or omission is in bad faith, and that any employee or agent of the adjudicator is similarly protected from liability.

(5)   If the contract does not comply with the requirements of subsections (1) to (4), the adjudication provisions of the Scheme for Construction Contracts apply.

Emphasis added.

As noted above, the Scheme for Construction Contracts, Part 1, Adjudication lays out the rules for adjudication where the contract terms do not meet the requirements of the Construction Acts. They are, in summary:

• Any party to a construction contract may give a written notice ('the notice of adjudication') at any time of their intention to refer any dispute arising under the contract to adjudication.
• The notice shall be given to every other party to the contract and shall include the nature and brief description of the dispute, the details of the parties involved, details of when and where the dispute arose and the nature of the redress which is sought.
• Compliance with the process for specifying the adjudicator, usually named or nominated by a named referring body, must be observed.
• The referring party sends the 'referral notice' to the adjudicator within seven days of the notice of adjudication, including the case pleaded and any documents relied upon.
• The adjudicator carries out their duties in accordance with the Act, acting fairly and investigating further if they so wish before delivering a decision.

- The adjudicator shall reach a decision not later than 28 days after receipt of the referral notice or 42 days after the receipt of the referral notice if the referring party agrees or any other period exceeding 28 days if both parties agree.
- The adjudicator's decision will be final, if agreed, or open to review in litigation or arbitration as appropriate. Costs will be allocated at the adjudicator's discretion, in accordance with the HGCRA 1996 as amended by the LDEDCA 2009.

Adjudication in practice

Almost any difference can be referred to adjudication as the wording of the Act is deliberately inclusive. As with all formal methods of dispute resolution it should be seen as a last resort after two-party discussions have achieved as much as they can.

"it should be seen as a last resort after two-party discussions have achieved as much as they can"

In practice, the usual procedure follows the Scheme above very closely, as would be expected when a very succinct piece of legislation is enacted. The process timetable could be as rapid as:

- written notice referring the dispute to adjudication (day 1);
- referral notice with documents to adjudicator (day 7);
- adjudicator's decision within 28 days (day 35).

Of course, the 28 days can be extended to 42 days with the referrer's consent, and other agreements can extend the time further, but the process is still quite rapid and is very intense. Many clients have complained that they have been hijacked by the process, with the referrer presenting a hugely complex or voluminous claim for them to defend in just a few days.

In 2005, I was faced with a referral which had to be answered in 21 days, and the referral included reams of paper supporting a £3 million claim for loss and expense and an extensive network programme showing an entitlement to 33 weeks' extension of time, none of which I had seen before. Luckily, by working long hours I was able to meet the deadline, arguing that a nine-week extension of time was the correct calculation for delay and that the claim for loss and expense was wholly unsubstantiated and so should be nil.

Fortunately, the adjudicator agreed with my analysis.

Section 10
Formal dispute resolution

In this Section:

- *Alternative dispute resolution*
- *Dispute resolution agents and boards*
- *Arbitration*
- *Litigation*

Alternative dispute resolution

In this *Good Practice Guide* series is a book called *Mediation* by Andy Grossman and so I refer you to that volume for a more in-depth study of the topic. In this section I cover the topic briefly in relation to loss and expense.

There are three main types of alternative dispute resolution (ARD) which may be used to resolve the evaluation of loss and expense: mediation, conciliation and the mini-trial. As a trained mediator who qualified in 1995 after being at the forefront of ADR since 1988, I believe that I am placing the three methods in order of popularity, at least with regard to the evaluation of loss and expense.

Mediation

In JCT Standard Building Contract with Quantities 2011, at clause 9.1, the parties are asked to give 'serious consideration' to mediation before embarking on any other method of dispute resolution. Much the same advice will be given to parties appearing before a judge under the pre-trial protocol, if they have not already attempted mediation.

In a typical mediation, an independent third party, the mediator, assists the parties through individual meetings with them ('caucuses') as well as in joint sessions. This 'shuttle diplomacy' is intended to allow the parties to focus on their real interests and strengths in a non-threatening environment. Each party is invited to make their case to the mediator confidentially, the mediator only disclosing that which they are asked to disclose to the other side. A mediator who is a skilled professional in the same industry may even be able to find flaws and weaknesses in the case as it is presented. This allows a strong mediator to point out probable challenges to the evidence from the other side before hearing from the other party.

"Disputes are often emotionally charged"

Disputes are often emotionally charged and lawyers have been known to be more emotional than the parties they are representing. The idea of speaking to the parties separately is to avoid the inevitable outpouring of emotion, in an attempt to draw the parties towards possible settlement.

Mediators do not ordinarily make recommendations as to what would be an appropriate settlement; their role is to assist the parties in finding a solution and reaching agreement between themselves. In this respect, under the Construction Acts, a mediator is very different from an adjudicator, who is called upon to make a decision.

Conciliation

Conciliators are usually less interventionist than are mediators but they still endeavour to bring disputing parties together and to assist them to focus on the key issues. Conciliation has been well-established in the United Kingdom in trade union and employment matters for a number of decades. The Advisory, Conciliation and Arbitration Service (ACAS) is active in the field of construction disputes and has a dedicated team for such disputes. Given the looseness of ADR terminology, the terms 'mediator' and 'conciliator' are often used interchangeably, although mediators do have a more active role than conciliators in construction matters.

Mini-trial

In this approach, which has many names, each party presents their case to the senior executives of both parties, who are often assisted by a neutral chairman. The parties may be represented by lawyers, although this practice has become less frequent in most cases. The chairman, perhaps a lawyer, judge or arbitrator, may advise on the likely outcome of litigation without any binding authority on the parties. After presentation of the issues, the executives try to negotiate a settlement. If successful, the settlement is often set out in a legally enforceable written document. The mini-trial is a misnomer to the extent that it is not really a trial as such. With the legal rules of evidence usually discarded and informality the norm, it is a settlement procedure designed to convert a legal dispute back into a business problem. In this respect the mini-trial clearly has a number of advantages:

• a lengthy hearing is eliminated
• each party's case can be professionally presented, but without any formal rules of procedure or evidence
• those who ultimately decide whether the dispute should be settled (and on what terms) have the opportunity to be guided by a person with some degree of prestige and objectivity
• the presentations are made to, and the ultimate decision made by, persons with the requisite authority to commit to settlement by the bodies which they represent
• costs are kept to a minimum.

Since 1990, ADR has been promoted in the United Kingdom by a number of bodies, including the Centre for Effective Dispute Resolution, the Academy of Experts and the Chartered Institute of Arbitrators, with varying degrees of success. Construction professionals disillusioned with the conventional processes of litigation and arbitration are unaccountably still reluctant to give mediation a chance. This is despite the fact that it has become extremely popular in other sectors and boasts a high rate of success.

Perhaps the construction industry is not yet ready for principled and independently led negotiations. It is indeed unfortunate that many contractor claims have now become so complex and inaccessible that even the contractors themselves are taken in by the clever, often logically superficial, formulations of their own claims consultants.

On the other side, many employers do not wish to pay or may have no money with which to pay. In such cases adjudication, arbitration or litigation then become equally attractive to both contractor and employer. The contractor believes that by means of a clever presentation they will be able to persuade an adjudicator, court or arbitrator of the legitimacy of their claim, while at the same time unscrupulous employers may view the slow and expensive legal process as a means of denying a contractor their legitimate and reasonable financial expectations.

Dispute resolution agents and boards

The purpose of a dispute resolution agent (DRA) or a dispute resolution board (DRB) is to enable loss and expense claims to be managed during the currency of the job. They are appointed before the work commences and are usually encouraged to keep up with the progress of the works, often by frequent site visits. Equally, they are encouraged to become familiar with the parties and personalities involved in the works.

Together, their knowledge of the people and the project will allow them to make informed decisions as to liability and costs. Such decisions allow the job to move on and the contractor to be paid for some loss and expense as the work proceeds, an invaluable aid to cash flow. As a general rule, the decisions of the DRAs and DRBs are not final; rather they can be opened up in arbitration later.

Where DRAs and DRBs are used, projects usually go more smoothly; fewer spurious claims are made and fewer genuine claims denied. The parties see a policeman and behave accordingly. In many cases decisions made by the DRAs and DRBs will not be challenged later and so, in effect, are final.

Architects and contract administrators on major projects may find it useful to factor in the use of 'in project' dispute resolution, perhaps recommending it to the employer and including it in the contract terms.

This type of dispute resolution presence is not inexpensive but it may provide value for money on a long-running and complex project faced with potential difficulties.

Arbitration

Most construction contracts, including all of those in the JCT, NEC and FIDIC stables, anticipate that dispute resolution will finally be referred to arbitration. JCT 2011 states at clause 9.3: 'Any arbitration pursuant to Article 8 shall be conducted in accordance with the JCT 2011 edition of the Construction Industry Model Arbitration Rules (CIMAR)'.

Of course the parties can agree to conduct their arbitration in accordance with the rules of any number of internationally accepted bodies. There are, for example, arbitrations held under the rules of the London Court of International Arbitration (LCIA), Dubai International Arbitration Centre (DIAC), International Chamber of Commerce (ICC) and UN Commission on International Trade Law (UNCITRAL). Many other countries and jurisdictions have their own equivalents. Clearly, if working internationally it is wise to use an internationally established body for arbitration to avoid any suggestion of bias.

Many construction professionals believe that arbitration has been hijacked by lawyers and turned into something akin to the litigation process in the High Court, and most of the international arbitrations in which I am involved are as formal and expensive as the court cases I attend. My older colleagues refer, wistfully, to an earlier period when arbitration was a cheap and quick method of dispute resolution, shorn of much of the paraphernalia of the legal process. I am sure that those days existed, but seemingly not for many years, according to the comment of Sir John Donaldson MR in *Northern Regional Health Authority v. Derek Crouch Construction Co. Ltd* (1984) when he noted that arbitration is 'usually no more and no less than litigation in the private sector'.

While some people crave a simpler form of arbitration, the fact is that much arbitration is extraordinarily complex and so the process is always likely to be complex too. Initiatives in the mid-1990s helped domestic arbitration to speed up and keep costs down but those measures mainly benefit relatively low-value, straightforward disputes.

Arbitration, like litigation, is essentially designed to identify and establish the legal rights and obligations of the parties; it is not a form of alternative dispute resolution. Construction disputes are usually complex,

"Arbitration is not a form of alternative dispute resolution"

not least those relating to loss and expense claims. Arbitral panels, apart from applying the law correctly to a given set of facts, also need to examine facts that interrelate and combine, determining where causation needs to be demonstrated and proved. Because construction disputes are complex, they rely heavily on witnesses of fact appearing before a judge or arbitrator and having their recollections and suppositions subjected to cross-examination. Too many claims in the construction industry commence on the basis that a project was programmed to complete in *x* weeks, only to be completed in *y* weeks. The contract value was £*x*, whereas the 'as built' costs were £*y*. The claimant then starts from the glib proposition that they are entitled to the difference between the contract value and the 'as built' cost as the direct loss and/or expense – a global claim by any other name.

The proper analysis of large and complex claims in the adversarial climate that arbitration shares with litigation is inevitably time consuming and expensive. For this reason, parties who commence arbitration thinking it is more cost effective than litigation may end up with a hearing of several weeks' duration or more and a costs bill of several hundred thousand pounds. In a case I was instructed on seven years ago, I was faced with a global claim that had approximately 650 lever-arch files of substantiation and very little summarisation. It took me a week to organise the files to follow the order of the pleadings. On a major power station dispute in the Midlands I worked in an 'arbitration war room' in a contractor's office block, reviewing over 2,000 files of costs, reports and programmes. Recently, in Dubai, I worked on a case where the quantum files alone numbered in excess of 4,500. Cases of this type will never be inexpensive to resolve under any methodology, except possibly ADR where generalised claims are made and met. I have often been involved in cases where the costs of the arbitration exceeded the sums in dispute; in such cases everyone loses.

Arbitration law and practice have long been part of the legal process. Since 1697 arbitration in England and Wales has been subject to legislative control. The present control is found in the Arbitration Acts 1950, 1975, 1979 and 1996.

It is for these reasons that attempts to speed up arbitrations are destined to falter. Nonetheless, and perhaps surprisingly, many procedural short-cuts, now common to litigation and arbitration, were in fact pioneered by the Official Referees in the High Court. These include exchange of expert witness reports, meetings of experts to agree 'figures as figures' and generally to identify those issues in the dispute that can be agreed and not agreed, and the exchange of statements by witnesses of fact.

Further modifications made by most arbitral panels include dispensing with opening and closing speeches other than in a written format, and allowing the witness statements of the lay witnesses to stand as evidence in chief. In addition, some arbitrators limit the time available to the parties to present their case, using a chess clock in some instances. However, whatever legitimate methods are adopted to limit the length of hearings, the need to test the evidence of the other party by detailed cross-examination can never be dispensed with, and this is probably the most time-consuming aspect of any trial or arbitration hearing.

There are other practical and logistical reasons for delays in concluding arbitrations. For example, counsel and expert witnesses, whose business is the process of litigation, are often unavailable to commence a hearing on a particular date, although they have considerable advance warning of the time commitments. Moreover, the lawyer's desire for more information by way of further and better particulars never appears to be fully satisfied. In all litigation, including arbitration, requests for further and better particulars (and replies to them), frequently difficult to resist, often delay the process of bringing the matter to trial or final hearing.

General arbitration procedure

Arbitration is now so widespread that parties who have contracted to use it rarely try to avoid it, although in the past many attempts were made to take disputes to the courts and bypass the agreed arbitration procedures. In such cases where litigation was commenced in the courts, the defendant would ask for a stay in proceedings to allow the arbitration to be held. Almost invariably a stay was granted and so now claimants rarely bother trying to bypass the arbitration agreement.

There is an excellent book on arbitration in this *Good Practice Guide* series called *Arbitration* by Dr Mair Coombes Davies, and I refer readers to that volume for a detailed analysis of the subject. Nonetheless, for completeness, I will provide a summary of how arbitration works for those seeking loss and expense and those defending against such claims. I will talk generally because all rules are different, but the substance of the process is similar across all rules.

Arbitrations, as noted above, are carried out under a set of rules agreed between the parties in the contract or afterwards. There are arbitrations that require a single arbitrator and some that require a panel of three (or more). Where a single arbitrator is required it is usual for a nominating body to recommend someone from a list; if this were not the case the agreement of who should be arbitrator might also require arbitration. Where a panel of three is required it is usually the case that each party chooses one member and the two chosen agree on a chairman.

Arbitrators are usually well-qualified, experienced and understand the law of the contract. Many are lawyers or former judges and a great number are engineers, architects or quantity surveyors. All will bring something to the arbitration that assists in achieving a positive outcome.

Hearings may be on documents alone or they may require witness evidence. Document-only arbitrations are cost effective but are not always suitable and so the greater proportion of arbitrations held will have hearings.

Once a notice of arbitration has been served, acknowledged and a tribunal has been appointed, a timetable will be agreed. It is worth remembering at this point that arbitration is a private arrangement between the parties and so without the consent of both parties it will become difficult for the tribunal to set timetables, order documents and resolve the dispute in hand. The timetable will typically set out the following:

- the date by which the claimant's case will be settled and pleaded
- the date by which the respondent will answer with a defence and a counterclaim
- the date by which the claimant will respond to the defence and defend the counterclaim
- the date by which any rejoinder(s) must be served to the tribunal and the other side
- the dates for exchange of witness statements and responses to witness statements
- the dates for the exchange of expert witness reports, along with the dates by which experts must have met and by which any joint statements should have been served
- the dates by which the arbitration bundles (the documents to be present in the hearing room) are to be settled and ready
- the dates of any intermediate and final hearings.

Naturally there will be flexibility in the dates and the tribunal will attempt to give the parties every opportunity to present their best case. The typical loss and expense claim is managed as follows.

The claimant prepares their pleading, which will look a good deal like the claim set out in Section 7 of this guie. The pleading should explain the obligation that was owed, how it was breached, the value of any loss incurred, the relationship of the loss to the breach and any special damage incurred, such as interest or financing. At this point in the proceedings, the claimant should present all of their arguments and evidence as it may well be their last chance.

As would be expected in any form of natural justice, the respondent is entitled to make a reply. The reply, or defence, should be equally well-founded, relying on facts and analysis, and it should be fully evidenced. While the burden of proof lies with the claimant, a poor defence that fails to address the claim fully may lead to a tribunal making an award on limited evidence. Again, the respondent should present all of their arguments and evidence or take the chance that it will be excluded. Should the respondent decide to make a counterclaim, the burden of proof for that counterclaim lies with the respondent. So, if the respondent is to succeed, they will follow the same pattern for proving the case as is laid out above for the claimant.

There will then follow a series of interactions demanding further information, clarity and more evidence, until finally the pleadings are settled and both sides know the case they are promoting and the one they are answering.

To support their respective cases the parties will use witnesses of fact to establish their allegations and to verify the facts as they have recorded them. Into the fray will be invited a number of expert witnesses (witnesses of opinion), who will be expected to comment on the validity of the facts and figures giving rise to the loss and expense sought on both sides. It is common for each side to appoint a quantum expert witness whose first responsibility is to the tribunal or the court and not to the party who pays them. This independence and impartiality is expected to bring commonality to the evaluation of the claims and to significantly narrow the quantum issues. The experts do not negotiate, nor do they decide liability, but they do try to agree how losses are to be measured and valued. They will then try to value them and arrive at the same answer, although this is rarely achieved.

I have been an expert witness for 20 years, have testified many times and have reported over 100 times on some very well-known structures and areas of infrastructure without ever losing a case. This is not because of my inherent brilliance, it is simply because I will encourage my client to settle if they are likely to lose. It is also because I will make every effort to be fair and cooperative with opposing experts, thus encouraging them to let their clients know if they are about to lose.

When all of the reports are in and the witness statements served, the hearing can begin. Often in a purpose-made arbitration room or a hotel ballroom, the tribunal will be dressed in suits and will take the head of the table. More often than not, at a 90-degree angle to the tribunal table will be two more tables seating the parties, who will face one another. Often the witnesses will be seated in between the two party tables, facing the tribunal as they give evidence.

Off to one side will be stenographers who record every word and who type every word simultaneously. In most cases now the transcript appears in real time on the computer screens of the parties and the tribunal.

The witnesses are asked to identify themselves and explain why they are qualified to give evidence to the tribunal. Usually they have witnessed something relevant to the breach or the expenditure of the cost incurred as a loss. Their printed statement, signed and verified, will usually act as their evidence in chief and the main questioning will be by the opposing counsel in cross-examination. The true purpose of cross-examination of factual witnesses is to undermine the credibility and integrity of the witnesses and so discredit their factual evidence.

Expert witnesses will be treated similarly, with their reports and joint statements being taken as read. In their case, the cross-examination is likely to be based on the differences between their report and the opposing expert's report. Opposing counsel will obviously try to undermine their opinion or convince them that the opposing expert's opinion is better or at least equally valid. The purpose of counsel's cross-examination is to sweep away the opposing expert's opinion, leaving counsel's own expert's opinion as the sole guide for the tribunal to consider when making an award.

When all of the evidence has been presented and the witnesses, of all types, have been examined, counsel for both parties will usually present, orally and in writing, a closing statement which summarises the evidence as they see it, stating why that evidence supports their case. They may also be bold enough to suggest to the tribunal a finding or series of findings that could be derived from the case. In any event they will remind the tribunal of their claims and their pleas for restitution and invite the tribunal to satisfy those claims in their award.

Once the case is over the hard work for the tribunal begins. They will try to come to a common view as to where liability lies and how any money claims for loss and expense should be valued. They will try to issue an award that is clear, well-reasoned and incapable of sensible appeal or challenge. Occasionally one member of the tribunal will dissent on an issue and that dissent will be recorded in the award.

Appeals against tribunal awards are rare and are equally rarely successful, the usual grounds being that:

- the tribunal lacked substantive jurisdiction
- the tribunal made an error of law
- the tribunal caused substantial injustice by some serious irregularity, perhaps by displaying a lack of natural justice or, more seriously, by its impropriety, such as taking a bribe.

Litigation

While the procedure for a major arbitration is very similar to a High Court litigation, the obvious difference is that the parties are inviting an organ of the state, the judiciary, to resolve their differences.

"the parties are inviting an organ of the state, the judiciary, to resolve their differences"

Essentially, the judge and the court are provided free of charge, although the parties can pay for additional stenography services, such as live feeds. The judges will usually be construction QCs who have worked in the courts for many years. They will try to list the case in the Technology and Construction Court (TCC), the headquarters of which is in Fetter Lane in London.

The parties will have to be represented by counsel able to practise in the UK courts and the judge and counsel will wear robes and possibly wigs. Some informality has crept into the TCC in the past two decades but customs and standards are still jealously guarded.

Judges are appointed to decide on matters of law and on disputed facts; many have little patience with parties who simply cannot agree what is sensible and so will refer parties to mediation or will suggest that the parties see whether they can reach an accommodation without troubling the court.

Witnesses are asked to affirm or to swear an oath and, once they are in the witness box, they cannot discuss the case with anyone, including their own counsel, until they are released. I was once in the witness box for seven court days, almost two weeks, and those were among the two most miserable weeks of my life, as my side kept well away from me for fear of being accused of tampering.

In most respects, and for a guide of this type, it would be safe for architects and contract administrators to assume that although the surroundings may be more imposing, or threatening, litigation will follow the pattern described earlier for arbitration.

On the topic of appeals, any appeal from a judge's decision must be specific and must be on a matter of law, not just an *appeal* for a second opinion because an outcome is seen as unacceptable. Such appeals can be granted by the trial judge giving leave to appeal, or by the Court of Appeal giving such leave.

SUMMARY

Formal dispute resolution is not fast; a typical case will take between one and two years to be heard from the start of proceedings. Further, the award or judgment can easily take a further nine months, and to suppose that a decision will be forthcoming in less than three months would be optimistic.

Formal resolution is costly; it involves many people who are at the top of their respective professions and who will be expensive. In 2011, it would not be unusual to see an expert witness charging £250 per hour, a lawyer £400 per hour and a QC £500 per hour. Of course, all of these individuals will have day rates and briefing fees which may reduce the hourly rate slightly, but this cannot be relied upon, even on a long-running case that lasts for months.

It is in the employer's interests for the architect or contract administrator and their quantity surveyor to resolve as many disputes as possible, even if that means allowing contract interpretations or valuations that favour the claimant.

Section 11
Good practice: loss and expense

In this Section:

- *Selecting the contract form*
- *Understanding the nature of claims*

Selecting the contract form

In my past experience of disputes, individuals have often chosen to use a specific, wholly unsuitable, form of contract simply because they were familiar with that form and its clauses. This is understandable but unacceptable. The contract form must be selected because of its suitability for the works and it must only be amended with care and expertise. Contract amendments should not be left to gifted amateurs; amendments should be made only by expert practitioners who know which clauses cause conflict and why. More importantly, these experts will know how to word contracts to offer maximum clarity and protection.

It is the legal obligation and responsibility of the architect or contract administrator to operate the contractual machinery independently and fairly. While the architect does not have a quasi arbitral role, the architect does have a professional duty to properly determine the liabilities of the contractor and employer for the purposes of certification.

Experience has shown me, as an expert witness, that disputes left to fester will quickly become incapable of early resolution. Fast action from the architect in valuing and certifying does three things: it shows everyone

"disputes left to fester will quickly become incapable of early resolution"

that the architect is exercising fairness in their dealings, it makes cash flow available to the contractor and it makes the remaining disputed sums less significant, perhaps too small to fight over.

Understanding the nature of claims

Recognising the difference between speculative or specious claims and valid claims is important, as is recognising the difference between contract claims and breaches of contract. If the architect and the project team do their level best to manage claims then there is little room for criticism. Expert witnesses will tell you that on too many occasions claims were set to one side because the architect did not understand them or was afraid of dealing with them. This guide is intended to instil such confidence in architects and contract administrators that they are able to face up to claims boldly.

By understanding what the law and the contract do and do not generally allow by way of recompense, the architect or contract administrator should be less fearful of money claims. Contractors and claims consultants will try to confuse and obfuscate, but a simple understanding of the principles taught in this guide will allow an architect to see through the fog of misdirection and make sensible allowances.

Understanding negotiation, adjudication and mediation will allow certifying professionals to concentrate on the case before them and not be concerned about procedure. Utilising these techniques with confidence will deflate spurious claimants and settle many loss and expense claims more quickly and cheaply than you might imagine.

No man is an island; not a single one of us has the monopoly on all information. Architects predominantly want to conceive, design, procure and complete projects which bring value to their society and they want to concentrate their efforts in that direction, and rightly so. People involved in the professions and whose day-to-day life does not revolve around disputes cannot be expected to be so knowledgeable that they will never need help. The wisdom of any person is most evident when they recognise that they need help. Once you have done all that you can, persuade your employer that an investment in assistance is both necessary and productive.

References

Table of legislation

Administration of Justice Act 1982
Arbitration Acts 1950, 1975, 1979 and 1996
Fraud Act 2006
Housing Grants, Construction and Regeneration Act 1996
Late Payment of Commercial Debts (Interest) Act 1998
Law Reform (Miscellaneous Provisions) Act 1934
Local Democracy, Economic Development and Construction Act 2009
Theft Act 1968

Table of cases

Berley Industries Inc. v. City of New York (1978)
Davy Offshore Ltd v. Emerald Field Contracting Ltd (1991)
F. G. Minter Ltd v. Welsh Health Technical Services Organisation (1980)
Hadley v. Baxendale (1854)
ICI plc v. Bovis Construction Ltd and Others (1992)
J. Crosby and Sons Ltd v. Portland Urban District Council (1967)
J. F. Finnegan Ltd v. Sheffield City Council (1988)
Jackson v. Barry Railway Company (1893)
John Doyle Construction Ltd v. Laing Management (Scotland) Ltd (2002)
John Mowlem v. Eagle Star Insurance (1992)
Lester Williams v. Roffey Brothers & Nicholls (Contractors) Ltd (1990)
London Borough of Merton v. Stanley Hugh Leach Ltd (1985)
Michael Salliss & Co. Ltd v. Carlil and William F. Newman & Associates (1987)
Mid Glamorgan County Council v. J. Devonald Williams & Partner (1992)
Northern Regional Health Authority v. Derek Crouch Construction Co. Ltd (1984)

Pacific Associates Inc. and Another v. Baxter and Others (1988) CA
Peak Construction (Liverpool) Ltd v. McKinney Foundations Ltd (1970)
Rees & Kirby Ltd v. Swansea City Council (1985)
Sutcliffe v. Thackrah and Others (1974)
Tate & Lyle Food and Distribution Ltd v. Greater London Council (1981)
Victoria Laundry (Windsor) Ltd v. Newman Industries Ltd (1949)
Walter Lilly & Company v. Giles Patrick Cyril Mackay, DMW Developments Ltd (2012)
Wharf Properties Ltd and Another v. Eric Cumine Associates (No. 2) (1991)

Bibliography and further reading

Birkby, G., Ponte, A. and Alderson, F. *Good Practice Guide: Extensions of Time*, RIBA Publishing, London (2008)

Coombes Davies, M. *Good Practice Guide: Arbitration*, RIBA Publishing, London (2011)

Dennys, N., Raeside, M. and Clay, R. *Hudson's Building and Engineering Contracts* (12th edn), Sweet and Maxwell, London (2010)

Duncan Wallace, I. N. QC, *Construction Contracts: Principles and Cause and Effect Policies in Tort and Contract* (out of print)

Grossman, A. *Good Practice Guide: Mediation*, RIBA Publishing, London (2009)

Hackett, M. and Trickey, G. *The Presentation and Settlement of Contractors' Claims*, Taylor and Francis, London (2000)

Horner, R. M. W. and Talhounie, B. T. K. *Effects of Accelerated Working, Delays and Disruption on Labour Productivity*, CIOB, Ascot (1996)

Latham, Sir M. *Trust and Money*, HMSO, London (1993)

Ramsey, The Hon. Sir V. and Furst, S. QC, *Keating on Construction Contracts* (9th edn), Sweet and Maxwell, London (2012)

Whitfield, J. *Conflicts in Construction*, Wiley Blackwell, Oxford (2012)

Index